SOCIAL IMPACT MARKETING

THE ESSENTIAL GUIDE FOR CHANGEMAKERS

MADDY KULKARNI

Kendall Hunt
publishing company

www.kendallhunt.com
Send all inquiries to:
4050 Westmark Drive
Dubuque, IA 52004-1840

To my mother, Hema, and my sister, Meera.

CONTENTS

INTRODUCTION

Who Is This Book For?

As a marketing professor, on the first day of each semester, I ask my students, "What do you think marketing is?" Inevitably, one bold and brave student will say what the others are thinking, "it's how you trick people into buying things!" Nervous laughter ensues. The students' eyes quickly dart back to me. I know what they're wondering: Is she cool enough to acknowledge we'll be studying the dark arts?

"Hmm . . .," I ask, "Well, let's say, hypothetically, that I'm a marketer at an automobile manufacturer. If I try to sell more of my new electric vehicles, ones that are better for the environment since they run on renewable energy versus fossil fuels, is that necessarily a bad thing?

"Or let's imagine I'm a marketer at a chocolate company. If I work to ensure my cocoa famers use sustainable farming practices and get paid a living wage, and I then put an "ethically sourced" label on my chocolate bars in the hopes people will choose my chocolate over other brands'— is that trickery?

"And what if I'm a passionate advocate of women's rights and I use social media to get the word out about a women's march? How do we feel about marketing that promotes social justice?"

I see the students' eyes get wide. I see them sit a bit straighter. I see a few smiles and I see some excitement. And perhaps I detect a slight disappointment that we won't be studying manipulation.

I started the Social Impact Marketing course at the University of Texas at Dallas in 2019 to teach students how marketing could be used as a force for good. Since it was a new course, a traditional textbook for the subject did not exist. As the saying goes, necessity is the mother of invention, and thus you have the book you are reading now.

There are two additional audiences I've had in mind while writing this book: nonprofit leaders and corporate brand managers. Through volunteering with nonprofits in my community, I've seen many not have the resources to dedicate towards marketing. It's hard to write a grant and secure funding for marketing efforts when donors want to see their dollars used directly for programming that helps people, not advertising. But what if marketing could help nonprofits reach and thus help more people? (Dan Pallotta has a thought-provoking TED Talk on this topic titled "The Way We Think About Charity is Dead Wrong.") Keeping the tight budgets in mind, the ten chapters in this book cover what I have seen to be the most essential and efficient marketing activities a nonprofit organization can take to drive impact.

On the other end of the spectrum, you have corporate brands managers with healthy marketing budgets. These marketers are learning however that traditional marketing must evolve. Consumers are expecting more from the brands they buy. They want to know if a brand's products are manufactured sustainably and if the workers who make them are treated fairly. Consumers seek brands that stand for something, that have purpose, because brands are a way consumers can express their values. 72% of Generation Z consumers (those born between 1997 and 2012) consider a company's purpose when deciding what to buy, and 83% of them say they consider it when deciding where to work.

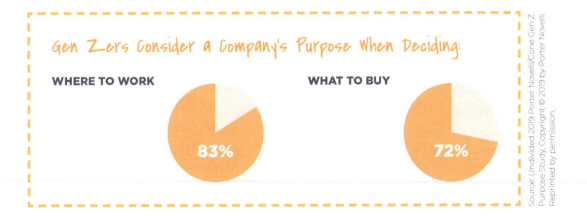

Source: Undivided 2019 Porter Novelli/Cone Gen Z Purpose Study. Copyright © 2019 by Porter Novelli. Reprinted by permission.

When large brands take on social and environmental issues, their size and scale have the power to drive systemic changes. But for brands to operate in more socially conscious ways, they will need new partners and new ways of working; this book will offer brand managers tools on how to navigate through this.

How Is Social Impact Marketing Different from Traditional Marketing?

Traditional marketing is the function of bringing a product to market where you have two primary goals: building brand equity and increasing sales. With social impact marketing you have a third goal: creating positive impact. This positive impact goal can be in service of environmental issues like reducing greenhouse gases, implementing regenerative farming practices, or cleaning up oceans and protecting watersheds. Or the positive impact goal could be in service of societal issues like advocating for gender and racial equality, providing safe water access, and ending hunger.

Here's a clever and powerful example of a social impact marketing campaign created by Lifebuoy, a soap brand owned by parent company Unilever. Lifebuoy realized that in developing countries, many diseases and even unnecessary deaths could be prevented by children learning to wash their hands properly. But they noticed kids weren't washing their hands long enough to kill germs. So Lifebuoy developed a liquid hand soap whose foam turns green after ten seconds, the time it takes to kill 99.9% of germs. In a cute 30 second advertisement of the product, you see a young boy playing with Marvel Comics' superhero the Hulk. When the young boy's mother asks him to wash his hands before eating a sandwich, he uses the Lifebuoy soap and watches the foam on his hands turn green. He imagines himself the Hulk and says "Germs! You'll be gone in ten seconds!" (*You can watch the video here:* http://bit.ly/Lifebuoy ColourChangingHandwash)

Even without sharing the financial results of the campaign, we can see how the three social impact marketing goals were achieved:

- ▶ The campaign built brand equity: Parents loved the product since it gave them proof their child was washing their hands for enough time.

- ▶ The campaign increased sales: The successful product launches in India and Indonesia led to expanding the product into other markets in Asia and Africa in 2013.

- ▶ The campaign created social impact: It encouraged a positive behavior change in kids to wash their hands long enough to kill germs, combating a leading cause of death for children under the age of five.

Do I Need to Have Taken a Marketing 101 Class to Understand This Book?

While it helps to have taken an introductory marketing course, it's not a requirement to understand and apply the concepts in this book. Social impact marketing concepts and best practices will be explained through many corporate and nonprofit campaign examples, and step-by-step instructions will be provided for how you can build marketing plans for your own product, idea, or organization.

How to Use This Book

I'm assuming you picked up this book because you are either in my class or you have an idea you think can make a social impact. Great! Use this book as a step-by-step workbook to develop the strategy for getting your idea to market. As you go through the chapters and exercises, you might find yourself wanting to edit and adjust things you worked on in previous chapters—I encourage you to do so! New thinking, research, and ideas will make your marketing plans stronger. When you get through the end of this book, you will have a robust marketing plan for your product or service.

If you don't have an idea for a product or service right now and want to read this book just for academic purposes, that's OK, but I think it'll be more fun if you pick an idea. Or pick an existing brand that you like, but that you feel has the power to do more good. Do the exercises in this book with that brand in mind and imagine yourself as the head of that brand's marketing department.

This book also is structured so you can enlist help from your friends and family. Many times, people will *want* to help you launch an idea, but they don't know *how* to help. With this book you can say, "Hey mom (or dad/sister/teammate/staff member/board member), can you help me with my social media strategy? Can you read up on Chapter 8?" or "Can you help me craft our PR strategy by reading through Chapter 9?"

Launching ideas that can change the world sounds daunting. This book attempts to break down the process into simple steps. I hope this book becomes a guide you can return to again and again whenever you have an idea you believe can help make the world a better place.

PART 1
THINK

Part 1 of this guidebook is about getting into the details of your social impact idea—what it is, who it serves, and the value it creates. You will also go through exercises that test and refine your idea. To do so, you will use traditional marketing frameworks, albeit with a social impact twist.

CHAPTER 1

5 P's Framework: Defining the Details of Your Idea

In this course, we are overachievers. As mentioned in the Introduction, we have two primary goals with traditional marketing: building brand equity and increasing sales. With social impact marketing however, we challenge ourselves with a third goal: creating positive impact. Given this ambition, right from the beginning of this book, we are going to take the first foundational framework marketers learn, the 4 P's Framework, and expand upon it by adding in a 5th P. Before diving deep into this 5 P's Framework though, let's reflect.

What typically happens when you get a great idea? You likely want to share it with the world, as soon as possible. This action of bringing a product or idea into the world ("to market") is called marketing. And when products or ideas are marketed for the purpose of social good you have social impact marketing. But shortly after the excitement of getting the idea, the next step—figuring out how to start telling people about it—can be overwhelming. Questions that might run through your head could include:

▶ *"Should I start by creating a logo? What should it look like?"*

▶ *"I want to fundraise for this cause. How can I create a viral video like the ALS Ice Bucket Challenge so I can raise donations?"*

> ▶ *"Should our team create a social media account on Instagram, Twitter, TikTok or whatever hot platform pops up next and try to get a million followers?"*

With so many possible approaches, a good strategy is to start with the basics. In his 1960 textbook *Basic Marketing: A Managerial Approach*, E. Jerome McCarthy introduced students to a simple 4 P framework to organize their thoughts around an idea. The 4 P's framework asks a student to capture details about an idea's **product, price, placement** and **promotion**. This framework is such a useful tool to get clarity about an idea, that not only is this framework still taught in schools today, it continues to be used by corporate marketing professionals responsible for billion-dollar brands. On top of those four fundamental P's, however, for social impact marketing we add a bonus 5th P for **partnerships**.

Here is a short explanation of the details each P nudges you to think through:

- ▶ **Product:** the attributes of a product or service you are trying to sell
- ▶ **Price:** how much you will charge for your product
- ▶ **Placement:** where people will be able to find your product
- ▶ **Promotion:** how you will tell people about your product
- ▶ **Partnership (the bonus P):** the people and organizations who will support the cause you are trying to advance with your product

The partnership P is essential to social impact marketing because not one product or organization can create lasting change by itself. To change behaviors, mindsets, and systems—to create social impact—requires the help and coordination of many people and organizations. In this book, we will talk a lot about the differences in how nonprofit and corporate organizations approach social impact. In practice, exponential impact can occur when nonprofits and corporate organizations work together. Nonprofits can expand their reach by benefitting from a corporation's scale, financial resources, and the business expertise of its employees. Moreover, corporations can benefit from a nonprofit's deep knowledge of a community or cause they are looking to make an investment in.

With this understanding of what the 5 P's framework entails, let's see it used in action. In Exhibit 1.1 you'll see the framework applied to an idea for a new sustainability club. Notice that simple bullet points work to capture the details of each P.

EXHIBIT 1.1   5 P's Framework for a New Sustainability Club

Product	▸ A Sustainability Club for students at University x ▸ Since the university has chapters in different cities (ex., the University of Texas has a chapter in Austin, Dallas, etc.) this club could be replicated in each of those cities if this first one becomes successful.
Price	▸ The financial cost to be a member of the club is free since this is a student organization. ▸ The organization will be funded through the university's Student Affairs budget. It will need $1,500 per year to cover the cost of pizza for monthly club meetings (10 meetings per year), T-shirts for the members, and a few other miscellaneous items.
Placement	▸ Club meetings will take place in building x on campus. ▸ Club activities (cleanups, recycling programs, etc.) will take place on the university's campus and sometimes throughout the city.
Promotion	▸ The club's founding members will attract students to join the club by: ▪ Putting up flyers around campus ▪ Creating a "Join Us" email they can forward to friends ▪ Adding the club's information on the university's website ▪ Participating in the club fair at the beginning of the school year
Partnership	▸ The club's leadership team will ask the Environmental Sciences professors to serve as advisors. ▸ It will also partner with the University's Facilities Management team so that the club's efforts are integrated in the recycling and composting processes for the campus.

That write-up didn't look too difficult, did it? To see the framework used for an idea in a corporate setting, check out Exhibit 1.2 for the 5 P's framework applied to an idea for a women's mentoring program.

EXHIBIT 1.2 5 P's Framework for a New Women's Mentoring Program

Product	A women's mentoring program at a corporation.
Price	▸ The program is funded by the corporation's Employee Resource Group's budget, which is managed by the Human Resources team. Funding will be used for guest speakers and snacks. ▸ The program is free to join. The "price" for participants is that both mentors and mentees commit to meeting for the mentoring sessions for a minimum of 30 minutes each month for 6 months. ▸ Managers of the mentors and mentees have agreed to allow the participants to spend 30 minutes per month during office hours for these meetings.
Placement	▸ Mentoring meetings will happen in the office or virtually during office hours.
Promotion	▸ An ad inviting women to join the mentoring program will be placed on the company's intranet website. ▸ Flyers about the program will be posted in break rooms. ▸ An email will be sent by Human Resources to all employees expressing its support of the program.
Partnership	▸ The mentoring program leaders will ask the Diversity, Equity & Inclusion team and the Talent Development team within the Human Resources function to serve as advisors for the program. ▸ The mentoring program leaders will also reach out to the local city chapter of the Lean In organization (www.LeanIn.org) for speaking engagements, consultation, and to stay connected on the latest learnings relevant to women in the workplace.

Does the exercise seem easy enough? Try it for a product or idea you think has the potential to make a social impact. Your idea can be for a new product, service, or organization. Or, your idea can be to build a more impactful version of something that already exists. Your idea can be scoped to benefit your local community or network, or it can be scoped to benefit your city, state, country, or the world. The only criteria in picking a social impact idea is that the intention of it should be rooted in creating a positive change for society.

EXERCISE 1.1 Draft a 5 P's Framework for Your Idea

Product	
Price	
Placement	

Promotion	
Partnership	

Now that you have taken a first stab at the 5 P's, generate the mindset of being open to continuously refining your original idea. To advance your thinking (we said we are overachievers in this subject!) use the questions below as prompts. One suggestion—draft the initial 5 P's, take a break, and then return to these questions when your mind is fresh.

▶ **Product:**

　　▶ Can you articulate three ***benefits*** your product or idea provides?

　　▶ Can you describe three ***features*** your product or idea has?

Note: Benefits are the *value* your idea brings, and features are *how* your idea provides those values. For example, with the packaging-free shampoo bars the handmade cosmetics brand Lush sells, the *benefits* of the product include helping the consumer make an environmentally friendly purchase, boosting hair's volume and increasing its shine. The *features* of the products include being packaging free, having a great scent, and being made with essential oils and fresh ingredients.

▶ **Price:**

　　▶ If your idea is for a physical product, do you want that product to be positioned as a premium, mainstream, or value product? If you want your product positioned as a premium product, what attributes would it need

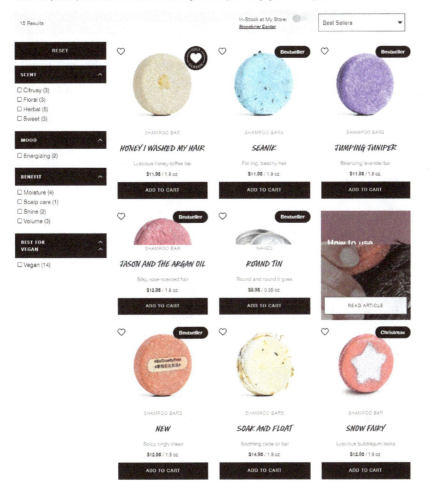

to justify its price for consumers? On the other end of the spectrum, if you want to offer a product at the lowest price point possible and increase its accessibility for lower income consumers, what product features can you reduce to make this possible?

▶ If your idea is for advocating a positive behavior change in society, what price will your consumer, or your company, have to pay? To illustrate this tradeoff, see how Tecate, a Mexican beer brand, decided to address rising gender violence, an act exacerbated when alcohol is involved. Tecate reported that in 2015, "two out of three women in Mexico suffer from some kind of gender violence and an astounding seven out of ten of them consider it normal." The brand partnered with the Mexican government on a bold campaign which included a video commercial with this voice-over: *"If you don't respect her, Tecate is not for you. We don't want you to buy us. Hopefully you will never find us."* While the brand was telling certain consumers not to buy their products, the campaign had great success in increasing positive sentiments towards the brand, winning creative excellence awards, and bringing awareness to the issue of gender violence. (*Watch the video here:* http://bit.ly/TecateMexico)

▶ What will make the funding of your idea sustainable, year after year? If your product is for an underserved, resource-constrained, low-income population, how will your product generate enough revenue to sustain your operations? Will there be someone who can provide initial (seed) funding? Will you look for a few large donors, or will you look to engage many donors who can donate small amounts of money?

▶ If you are looking to raise donations to fund your operations, can you easily explain what the donations will be used for? For example, if you run a temporary housing service, can you share how a $200 donation will help a family of four cover groceries for one week and that a $50 donation will cover internet expenses for one month?

- **Placement:**

  - What geography does your idea or product serve? Where could it expand to?

  - Where is the easiest place for people to access your product or services? Can they engage with you online, in person, or in both ways?

- **Promotion:**

  - In what ways can you get the word out about your idea? Can you leverage social media, email, churches, conferences, or partners' email newsletters?

  - In what ways can you attract new customers and donors while also keeping your existing customers and donors engaged?

- **Partnerships:**

  - Map out as many players and organizations you can think of in the ecosystem of your cause area—how many of them can you partner with (in varying degrees)? For example, if you are trying to increase diversity in the advertising industry, you'd likely want to partner with companies that spend significant dollars on advertising, creative agencies, media outlets, consumer advocacy organizations, and many others to bring about this change.

  - Amongst your partners, can you establish common metrics to measure collective progress against a cause? For example, if an after-school tutoring program reports its impact through an improvement in test scores, and another after-school tutoring program reports its impact based on the number of hours it's able to offer each student, and another reports on an improvement in the number of disciplinary incidents of students in their program, it is difficult for a school district to compare and measure the effectiveness of the programs. If each of the tutoring programs agree to report on the same metrics, progress and impact become easier to measure.

These questions are intended to serve as thought starters. See in Exhibit 1.3 how they can be used to advance the thinking on the idea for a sustainability club that was introduced previously.

EXHIBIT 1.3   An ***ADVANCED*** 5 P's Framework for a New Sustainability Club

Product	▸ A Sustainability Club for University x
	▸ Since the university has chapters in different cities (ex., the University of Texas has a chapter in Austin, Dallas, etc.) this club could be replicated in each of those cities if this first one is successful.
	▸ The club will allow students to accumulate community service hours which are a requirement for graduation.
	▸ The club will teach students on how to implement more environmentally sustainable practices while making a positive environmental impact on their school's campus.
	▸ The club will organize sustainability-related community service events (two times per year), host an (annual) Earth Day campus event, and bring in speakers to talk about careers in sustainability (four speakers per year).

Price	▶ The financial cost to be a member of the club is free since this is a student organization.
	▶ The organization will be funded by the university's Student Affairs budget. It will need $1,500 per year to cover the cost of pizza for monthly club meetings (10 meetings per year), T-shirts for the members, and a few other miscellaneous items.
	▶ To ensure funding from Student Affairs year after year, the club will maintain an active membership of a minimum 50 students and create three events per year that are open to the entire university.
	▶ Members will receive their club T-shirt after completing 10 community service hours with the club.
Placement	▶ Club meetings will take place in building x on campus. Club activities (cleanups, recycling programs, etc.) will take place on the university's campus and sometimes throughout the city.
	▶ The club members will engage with the personnel of the city's recycling center which is ~3 miles from campus. The club will also engage with the personnel of the on-campus composting site.
	▶ For events that feature speakers, in-person attendance is preferred, however, these events will be recorded or live streamed for those students who cannot attend.
Promotion	▶ The club's founding members will attract students to join the club by:
	■ Putting up flyers around campus
	■ Creating a "Join Us" email they can forward to their friends
	■ Adding the club's information on the university's website
	■ Participating in the club fair at the beginning of the school year
	▶ The club will remind members to come to meetings and events by sending out email and text reminders. It will also remind members that they get community service hours, a requirement for graduation, by participating in club activities.
	▶ Members will be encouraged to wear their club T-shirts during key campus events like Welcome Weekend and Earth Day celebrations to generate more awareness of the club.

Partnership	▸ The club's leadership team will ask the Environmental Sciences professors to serve as advisors.
	▸ It will also partner with the University's Facilities Management team so that the club's efforts are integrated in the recycling and composting processes for the campus.
	▸ The club will connect with an external environmental footprint measurement organization to get advice on how to measure the club's impact. From this organization, members of the club will techniques to:
	■ Measure the amount of plastic deferred from landfill as a result of the club's efforts, and
	■ Determine soil quality improvement at a nearby farm from using compost created from the campus organic waste.

After reading through this expanded example, revisit your own 5 P write-up in Exercise 1.1. See if you can expand on your initial thinking.

You will return to edit your 5 P's a few times as you complete more exercises in this book. Your idea will likely evolve to include perspectives from the different people you show it to. Your idea should evolve with time as well, as people's familiarity and acceptance of it grows.

Now you know how to apply the most basic of marketing frameworks to ideas for social impact. Turn to this framework as a first step any time you get an idea that has potential to make the world a better place.

CONNECTING THE DOTS

By completing the 5 P's Framework in this chapter, you now have a clear articulation of *what* your social impact idea is about. This is an important foundational step to marketing your idea. In Chapter 2, you will work on clearly defining *who* your idea serves. This will help focus your marketing efforts on reaching the people who most need to hear your message.

CHAPTER 2

3 C's Framework: Defining Who Your Idea Serves

You've sharpened your idea in Chapter 1 and now you're ready to get very clear on who your social impact idea is going to serve. While the first chapter concentrated on your *product*, this second chapter will focus on *people*, specifically the people your product will help and the people you will work with closely to bring your product to market. To help us do this, we'll be looking at another frequently used marketing framework, the 3 C's, but again, we're going to add our social impact marketing spin to it.

When generating your social impact idea, you likely had someone in mind who your product or service would be helping. You likely started thinking about what resources you'd need to bring that idea to life. And you likely started thinking about which organizations might be doing similar work. These thoughts about your *consumers*, your *company*, and your *competition* make up the elements of organizational theorist, Kenichi Ohmae's 3 C's framework. Introduced in his book *The Mind of the Strategist: The Art of Japanese Business,* this 3 C's framework is another widely popular tool used by marketers worldwide. In a very simplified explanation, here is what each C entails:

- ▶ **Consumer or Customer:** This C addresses the people who *use* (or "consume") your products—these are your consumers. It also addresses the people who *buy* your products—these are your customers. Sometimes a product's consumers and customers are different entities, and sometimes they are the same. Therefore, we group them into one C in the framework.

- ▶ **Company:** This C addresses the capabilities of the people and operations of your organization.

- ▶ **Competition:** This C addresses who you are up against to gain consumers and customers.

We'll be studying each of these 3 C's in depth. But a quick spoiler—we'll be challenging this third C on competition. In traditional marketing, companies try to win in the marketplace by stealing market share and beating the competition. In social impact marketing however, remember that winning is not the goal. Beating the competition is not the goal. The goal is to create a positive impact. So why compete? Our social impact goals like climate change, gender equality, and hunger, are too large for one organization to solve alone. So why not start seeing traditional competitors as *collaborators?* There is enough work to be done, and we'll achieve our goals if we work together more efficiently. Case in point, even PepsiCo and Coca-Cola, two companies traditionally seen as fierce competitors in the carbonated beverage category, collaborate on efforts to drive up recycling rates and end plastic waste pollution. As members of The Recycling Partnership, they jointly invest in launching more neighborhood curbside recycling programs, resident outreach efforts, and contamination prevention education so that plastic and other materials are recycled in their correct recycling streams.

From this introduction to the 3 C's, let's look to a beautiful case study of how the team at furniture retailer IKEA might have used the framework to evaluate a social impact idea around products for the physically disabled. In Israel, Eldar Yusupov, a copywriter with cerebral palsy at IKEA's advertising agency McCann Tel Aviv, had an idea for small hacks that would make IKEA furniture more accessible. Consumers with cerebral palsy for instance, have trouble getting up from conventional sofas, have trouble opening regular closet doors, and have trouble turning on lamps with small switches. A set of risers that could be attached to existing IKEA sofas could make them easier to get up from. When deliberating if "add-on" products like these risers was a viable idea, IKEA's marketers could likely have had this thought process:

- ▶ **Consumers:** Research showed that 10% of Israel's population have physical disabilities that prevent them from easily using regular furniture. Add-ons that could easily connect to IKEA's existing products could help them serve new consumers.

- ▶ **Company:** This idea connected strongly to advancing the company's mission around "democratizing IKEA furniture and making them accessible for all." And while the products were first launched in Israel, IKEA's website offered free downloadable files making these add-on products accessible for 3D printing anywhere in the world.

- ▶ **Competition:** The existing furniture offerings for people with disabilities were expensive and not very stylish. In this case, IKEA likely did not have to collaborate with these competitors since it had access to its own product designers.

- ▶ **Collaborators:** IKEA could (and did) collaborate with nonprofits Access Israel and Milbat who specialize in creating products for people with disabilities.

IKEA launched the idea in 2019 with the ThisAbles campaign and successfully hit all three social impact marketing goals:

- ▶ The campaign built brand equity: Measured sentiments towards IKEA's brand in categories of "a genuine value-led business," "innovation," and "supports local communities" all saw significant increase.

- ▶ The campaign increased sales: In 2019, IKEA saw a 37% sales increase of products with add-ons (vs. 2018).

- ▶ The campaign created social impact: The products are now being downloaded around the world and can impact the 900,000 Israelis and 700 million people globally with physical disabilities.

Watch the video here: http://bit.ly/SocialImpactMktgThisAbles
Watch a behind the scenes look at how the campaign came together here:
http://bit.ly/IKEABehindtheScenes

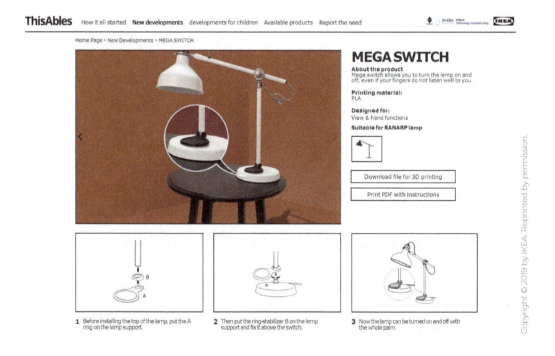

Are you inspired? Are you ready to apply the 3 C's to your social impact idea? Let's get started and approach each of the 3 C's step by step.

Consumers and Customers

Previously, we mentioned there is an important distinction between a product's consumers and customers—sometimes they are the same entity, and sometimes they are different. Here's an example where a product's consumer and customer are the *same*: A cosmetics brand creates a new lipstick line that is vegan and is certified cruelty-free by PETA (People for the Ethical Treatment of Animals). An eco-conscious woman who buys the lipstick for herself is both the consumer and the customer.

Here's an example where the consumer and customer are *different*: A food production company creates nutritious meals that can be easily shipped and cooked in areas affected by natural disasters. The consumer is a resident in the affected area who needs the meals. The customer is usually an organization, such as the World Food Programme, which purchases and then distributes the meals to the residents in need.

Each entity in this example has different needs or ***problems to solve.*** The consumer needs meals that are satiating and easy to cook with limited resources. The customer needs nutritious and culturally appropriate meals (e.g. vegetarian for some markets) that are easy to transport and unpack. Marketers spend a significant amount of time getting to know their consumers' and customers' problems to solve so they can create products that serve these needs. Check out Exhibit 2.1 for another example of differences between the problems to solve of consumers and customers, this time with a backpack meal program that provides the third meal of the day to send home with students after school.

EXHIBIT 2.1   Consumers, Customers, and Their Problems to Solve for a Backpack Meal Program

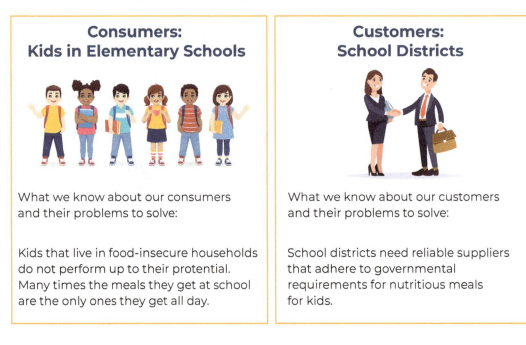

Consumers:
Kids in Elementary Schools

What we know about our consumers and their problems to solve:

Kids that live in food-insecure households do not perform up to their protential. Many times the meals they get at school are the only ones they get all day.

Customers:
School Districts

What we know about our customers and their problems to solve:

School districts need reliable suppliers that adhere to governmental requirements for nutritious meals for kids.

After reading these examples, think about how you can define the consumers and customers for the social impact idea you started building in Chapter 1. Throughout this book, do the exercises with that idea in mind.

EXERCISE 2.1 Describe Your Idea's Consumers, Customers, and Their Problems to Solve

Consumers:	Customers:
[Insert or draw a picture of your consumer]	[Insert or draw a picture of your customer]
What we know about our consumers and their problems to solve:	What we know about our customers and their problems to solve:

In Chapter 4 we will discuss how to conduct in-depth research on your consumers and customers which will help you further define their problems to solve. But for now, let's move on to diving deeper into the second C of the framework.

Company

Taking a realistic look at your organization's capabilities can help you assess if you have the necessary people and resources in place to execute your idea. We will approach this assessment by:

1. Evaluating how closely different functions work together within a corporation and the experience of the leadership team in a nonprofit

2. Confirming that members of the organization are aware and are aligned to its purpose, mission, and future goals

3. Understanding the organization's strengths, weaknesses, opportunities and threats

Firstly, given the size and scale differences between corporations and nonprofits, let's look at how each might approach accessing the capabilities of their teams in tackling social impact issues. Traditionally, in corporations, the marketing departments work quite independently from the HR (human resources) and sustainability teams. Now however, as consumers expect brands to operate in more socially conscious ways, marketers must engage with these functions more closely to answer these types of consumer questions:

▶ What is the brand doing to combat human rights issues in its supply chain?

▶ Are the brands' workers getting paid fair wages? Are they working in safe environments?

▶ Are the brand's products made with sustainable packaging?

- ▶ Are the ingredients in the brand's products sustainably sourced?

- ▶ What is the brand's carbon footprint?

If you are a corporate marketer, ask yourself, "Do I know the people who lead diversity, equity, and inclusion (DEI) in my HR department? Do I know the people in our sustainability team? Can I set up monthly or quarterly meetings with them to ensure that not only are DEI and sustainability efforts embedded into the way my products are made, but also that I can talk to my consumers about these efforts in an accurate way?"

Let's now shift a bit and think through how a nonprofit might approach accessing the capabilities of its leadership team. Reflect on the experiences the founder, key staff members, and board members bring to the work that could build the confidence volunteers, program recipients, and donors have in the organization. Laying this information out in a simple write up as per Exhibit 2.2 can help you see at a glance what expertise your organization's team currently possesses.

EXHIBIT 2.2 A Backpack Meal Program's Leadership Team and Their Qualifications

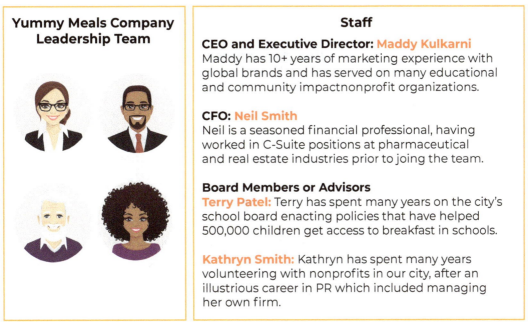

Yummy Meals Company Leadership Team	Staff
	CEO and Executive Director: Maddy Kulkarni Maddy has 10+ years of marketing experience with global brands and has served on many educational and community impactnonprofit organizations.
	CFO: Neil Smith Neil is a seasoned financial professional, having worked in C-Suite positions at pharmaceutical and real estate industries prior to joining the team.
	Board Members or Advisors **Terry Patel:** Terry has spent many years on the city's school board enacting policies that have helped 500,000 children get access to breakfast in schools.
	Kathryn Smith: Kathryn has spent many years volunteering with nonprofits in our city, after an illustrious career in PR which included managing her own firm.

Images © Volha Hlinskaya/Shutterstock.com

Take some time to fill out the chart in Exercise 2.2 for your organization's team. (This content can be repurposed in Chapter 6 for the website's About Us page you will build.)

EXERCISE 2.2 List Members of Your Organization's Leadership Team and Their Qualifications

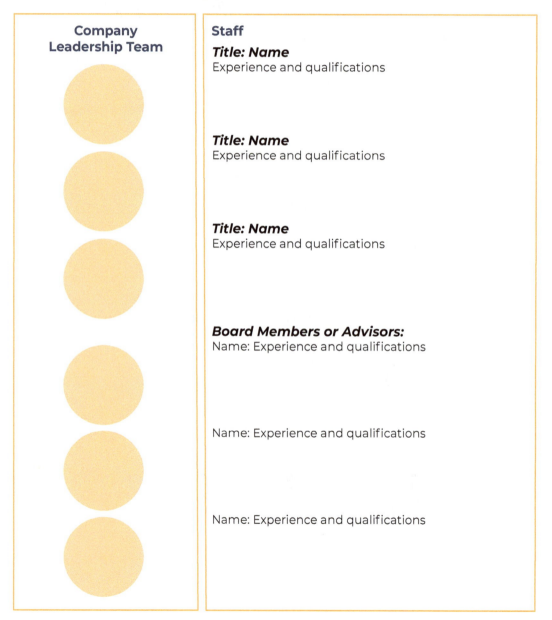

Company Leadership Team	Staff
	Title: Name Experience and qualifications **Title: Name** Experience and qualifications **Title: Name** Experience and qualifications **Board Members or Advisors:** Name: Experience and qualifications Name: Experience and qualifications Name: Experience and qualifications

Review if there are any functional areas missing from your leadership team's expertise. Could your organization benefit from hiring someone where there currently might be gaps? Do you have representation from the critical functions your business requires—perhaps marketing, supply chain, human relations, public relations, technology, legal, and/or public policy? And speaking of representation, it is important to reflect on the diversity of your team. Does it reflect the communities you serve? If it doesn't, think through ways you might expand your network to include those voices on your team.

Our next step is to ensure that members of the organization's team are clear and aligned to its purpose, mission, and future goals. Notice the nuances between purpose and mission through the example in Exhibit 2.3.

EXHIBIT 2.3 A Backpack Meal Program's Purpose, Mission, and Future Goals

Purpose (Why our organization exists): We exist so that hunger doesn't limit children reaching their full potential.

Mission (What our organization does): We send students home with a third meal of the day in their backpacks, so that they are guaranteed a nutritious dinner when they leave school.

Future Goals: While currently in two school districts in the Houston metroplex, we plan to expand to three more school districts within the next 3 years.

In collaboration with your teammates, crystallize the language for your organization's purpose and mission and align on one to three future goals. Capture them on the following page in Exercise 2.3.

EXERCISE 2.3 Write the Purpose, Mission, and Future Goals for Your Organization

Purpose (Why our organization exists):

Mission (What our organization does):

Future Goals:

In the third step of our assessment, we will think through our company's strengths, weaknesses, opportunities, and threats through a SWOT analysis. Note that strengths and weaknesses are internal to a company, while opportunities and threats are external elements that can affect a company. See an example of a SWOT analysis in Exhibit 2.4.

EXHIBIT 2.4 A Backpack Meal Program's SWOT Analysis

Strengths	Weaknesses
▸ Our strong network with religious organizations and corporations means we have a steady number of accessible volunteers. ▸ We have an experienced logistics staff.	▸ We do not have someone with marketing expertise on our board or staff. ▸ We have yet to develop menu items that integrate favorite dishes of the refugee children in our district.
Opportunities	**Threats**
▸ Hunger has recently been chosen as a priority cause by two prominent foundations in the city, so additional grants and funding opportunities may become available. ▸ Backpack manufacturing companies have reached out to sponsor/donate backpacks. ▸ Outside organizations have asked to use our kitchen during our non-working hours. This might lead to a new revenue stream for us.	▸ Bread for sandwiches is donated by two local restaurants but isn't guaranteed. ▸ The government might release updated dietary guidelines next month which might require changing some menu items.

While the example only has a few bullet points in each box, try to spend time thinking through as many points as you can for the SWOT you create in Exercise 2.4. The more thoughtful you can be on getting a clear picture here, the more creative you can get with your marketing activations.

EXERCISE 2.4   Create a SWOT Analysis for Your Organization

Strengths	Weaknesses

Opportunities	Threats

Competition and Collaborators

In this third C of the 3 C's framework, we are again going to be overachievers in the attempt to turn our traditional competitors into collaborators. Sure, healthy competition can be good. It can help galvanize and motivate a team to work harder to win against a common enemy. But in social impact marketing, when you are trying to solve environmental and societal issues, the enemy is bigger than your competition. The enemy can be challenges like access to clean water, quality education, and criminal justice reform. Fighting enemies like these require the collaboration of many people and organizations.

In addition to the PepsiCo and Coca-Cola recycling collaboration mentioned previously, here are two more examples of how this could work. In the social media space, might competitors like Facebook, Twitter, YouTube, and other platforms come together to eliminate cyber bullying and the proliferation of misinformation? Could they develop standards, tools, and processes the entire industry could adopt? In the nonprofit sector, might a school district and a homeless shelter apply for a grant together to turn an unused school building into a drop-in center with residential services for homeless teens? Recall the problems to solve for your consumers and think through creative collaborations around solutions you might not be able to implement alone.

So take inventory—which brands or services are competing with you for grants, donors, or market share? Where might you be able to collaborate? Review the questions and example in Exhibit 2.5 to help you brainstorm opportunities for your company.

Logos or Names of Competitors/ Potential Collaborators

What do similar organizations do well that our organization won't or can't?
Other school meal programs provide milk in their meal kits, but given refrigeration requirements of the organic milk we'd like to provide, we can't do that yet.

What are similar organizations doing that we'd like to do as well?
Similar organizations sometimes send extra school supplies in the backpacks. We can do the same when those items are donated to us.

Where could our organizations partner together to expand our reach?
(Ex. Could you split up the geographies you serve? Could you share learnings and best practices? Can you jointly develop a list of metrics you will measure so that there's more data around the cause you are working on?)

We could partner on data tracking—if we all measure the same metrics and show that the backpack meal programs result in higher test scores, fewer behavioral issues, and other success metrics for the children participating, it could help all the third meal backpack programs secure more funding from the state government.

What other problems to solve do our consumers have that we might be able to help with?
Many of our students have younger siblings that don't attend school yet. We should figure out how and who could help us reach these kids with nutritious meals.

You know the drill now, give the exercise a try!

EXERCISE 2.5   Brainstorm How Your Current Competitors Can Become Collaborators

Logos or Names of Competitors/ Potential Collaborators	
	What do similar organizations do well that our organization won't or can't?
COMPANY LOGO	
COMPANY LOGO	What are similar organizations doing that we'd like to do as well?
COMPANY LOGO	
	Where could our organizations partner together to expand our reach?
	What other problems to solve do our consumers have that we might be able to help with?

In summary, this understanding of the social impact marketing 3 C's can help you stay focused as you evaluate ways to build the idea you developed in Chapter 1. If someone suggests new features to your product for instance, you can ask yourself, "Do these new features serve my consumer? Do I have the right experience on my team to build these new features? Does my competition have these features, and could I ask them to collaborate with me on them?"

CONNECTING THE DOTS

After you have completed the 3 C's exercises in this chapter, take a few moments to go back to Chapter 1 to review your 5 P's. Are there different ways you would handle the price or promotion of your idea given you now have a deeper understanding of your consumer and customer? After looking at potential collaborators, are there any new partnerships you'd like to explore? Understand that marketing is an iterative process. New learnings should influence how you adjust, evolve, and then market your ideas.

CHAPTER 3

STP Framework: Defining Your Idea's Value

Think about a gift you've received and loved. Why was it so special? It was likely because the gift felt personal and thoughtful, like the person who gave it to you took the time and effort to understand you and figure out what you might like. This is the feeling you want to generate in consumers when they buy your product—that it was built especially with them in mind. Contrast this with the notion that you'd probably like your idea to reach as many people as possible. But if you're trying to reach as many people as possible, how do you make each person feel unique, feel special?

This is where the steps in the Segmentation, Targeting, and Positioning (STP) framework come to the rescue. This framework guides you through defining the consumers you serve more precisely, so that you can determine and articulate the value you wish to create for them. At a high level, here is what happens in each step of the framework:

- ▶ **Segmentation:** This is the first step when you brainstorm all the different ways you can group your consumers or customers, based on similar needs.

- ▶ **Targeting:** This is the second step when you choose a few segments (usually two to three) to focus your marketing efforts on.

- ▶ **Positioning:** This is the final step when you articulate the unique benefits and value your product brings to your chosen targets.

This "value" in a product's positioning is a differentiating element between traditional marketing and social impact marketing. In traditional marketing, a product's value to a consumer could be functional, or it could be for status or entertainment. For example, a banana's function could be to curb a consumer's hunger. A luxury car's function could be to help someone feel important. And an action movie's function can be to entertain. In social impact marketing however, a product's value includes helping the consumer be a part of a movement, a part of change. An organic banana helps a consumer make a choice that supports sustainable agriculture practices. An electric luxury car helps a consumer show to the world she's "made it" but that she also cares about the environment. A movie in which the lead male and lead female actors get paid equally helps advance the dialog and movement towards gender equality.

A fun example in which we can see the STP framework come to life is in the "Love the Change" campaign by Pampers, the baby diapers brand owned by parent company Procter & Gamble. Initially, the brand could have described its consumers as "parents." But there are hundreds of millions of parents in the world, which would be hard to connect with in a single campaign. Therefore, Pampers could have segmented parents into groups, such as first-time parents, single parents, mothers, fathers, adoptive mothers and fathers, foster parents, Asian parents, Hispanic parents—the list can get long. Out of all these groups, Pampers decided to choose fathers as their target in 2019.

In the commercial for "Love the Change," the company featured superstar singer-songwriter John Legend changing the diaper of his baby boy, Miles. While changing the diaper, he starts singing a tune, "somebody's got a stinky booty—whoo!" He calls for "backup" and a full entourage of about twelve men carrying their own babies appears and joins in on the tune. Then Legend is joined by Adam Levine, his co-host on the show *The Voice*, who sings the last line of the tune very sweetly while changing his own baby's diaper, "and daddy's gonna clean it up." At the end of the commercial, Chrissy Teigen, author, supermodel, and Legend's wife, enters, car keys in hand, and asks, "Must we do this every time?" Legend smiles, shrugs, and the ad ends. The commercial is playful, has a superstar cast, and conveys a message to men to "be a part of this movement, fathers have a role to play in changing diapers." (*Watch it here:* http://bit.ly/PampersLovetheChange)

Through this campaign, Pampers positions itself as a brand that advocates for progressive gender roles, with a product both mothers and fathers can use to bond with their babies. Fathers will hopefully see the commercial and think, "OK, I'm not the only father here who changes diapers. This can be fun and 'my boys' are with me on this journey. Pampers understands me." The ad feels personal and hence the consumer develops an emotional connection to the brand.

Let's now go a bit deeper into each step of the STP framework and practice using it for our ideas.

Segmentation

In the segmentation step, your goal is to create as many groups of your consumers as possible. Consider differences in gender, geography, psychographics, ages, and abilities to help you create the groups. In Exhibit 3.1 notice how two organizations, a senior living center and an indoor vertical farming company, create segments for their consumers.

EXHIBIT 3.1 Segmentation of Consumers and Customers

Senior Living Center Consumer Segments	Indoor Vertical Farm Consumer and Customer Segments
 © wavebreakmedia/Shutterstock.com  © Monkey Business Images/Shutterstock.com	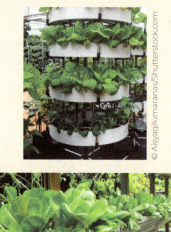 © Aisyaqilumaranas/Shutterstock.com © Aisyaqilumaranas/Shutterstock.com (Note: *Consumers* would be the people who eat the produce and *Customers* would be people who purchase the produce or vertical farm equipment)
1. Single seniors 2. Married senior couples 3. Seniors with pets 4. Seniors who need significant medical attention 5. Seniors who need very little medical attention 6. Seniors with significant mobile constraints 7. Seniors who are single but would like a roommate 8. Seniors who drive 9. Seniors who want to be able to cook in their apartments 10. Seniors whose families live far away	1. People who garden as a hobby 2. Local organic and/or high-end restaurants 3. Local school districts 4. Charter or private schools 5. Local grocery stores 6. Manufacturers of packaged vegetables 7. Food banks 8. Corporate offices that have cafeterias 9. People who like to shop at farmers' markets 10. Local hospitals

Again using the same social impact marketing idea you have been working through in Chapters 1 and 2, try creating at least 10 segments into which you could group your product's consumers and note them in Exercise 3.1.

EXERCISE 3.1   Create Segments of Consumers and/or Customers for Your Social Impact Idea

Consumer and Customer Segments
1.
2.
3.
4.
5.
6.
7.
8.
9.
10.

Targeting

Let's move forward to the second step of the STP Framework, targeting. Given that you likely have some limit to the time and money you can spend on marketing, choosing two to three segments as your targets helps you create more meaningful and impactful campaigns. Here are some considerations when picking your top three segments:

- ▶ Which segments are the largest?

- ▶ Which segments have the most potential for growth?

- ▶ Which segments will be the easiest for you to create something unique and valuable for?

In addition to these questions, for a social impact idea, you might also want to ask:

- ▶ Which segments of the population have been traditionally *underserved*?

In the Pampers example, even though women have traditionally been the largest segment of primary caregivers to children, Pampers decided to target men, a group who had yet to be marketed to in this product category.

Here's another example of how a brand targeted a traditionally underserved group—veterans. Former U.S. Defense Secretary Robert M. Gates pointed out a problem with how corporate America was viewing veterans. "One of the most significant challenges our veterans face is a corporation's inability to understand and translate the skills of military service into a meaningful private sector role," Gates said. He went on to underscore that, "Veterans and military spouses represent one of the most underutilized talent pools in our country and, without the proper career path, will continue to go untapped." Howard Schultz, chairman, president and chief executive officer, of Starbucks, the global coffee brand, saw the opportunity. "The more than one million transitioning U.S. veterans and almost one and one-half million military spouses—with their diverse background and experience—share our mission-driven sensibility and work ethic," he said, "and can build long-term careers at Starbucks as they return home." In 2013, Starbucks, committed to hiring 10,000 veterans and active duty spouses as the service men and women transitioned back to civilian life in the U.S. Starbucks set a five year timeline to achieve this goal, and it met the commitment one year early! It has since made a commitment to hire 5,000 veterans and military spouses yearly.

When looking at which segments you want to target with your social impact idea, take cues from the previous examples by asking yourself, "what is an underserved segment we can help while also having a positive impact on our business?"

Now, returning to the exercise for the senior living center and the indoor vertical farm, see how the top three segments we have chosen to focus on are circled in Exhibit 3.2.

Exhibit 3.2 Choosing Targets from a Variety of Segments

Senior Living Center	Indoor Vertical Farm
1. Single seniors	1. People who garden as a hobby
2. Married senior couples	2. Local organic and/or high-end restaurants
3. Seniors with pets	3. Local school districts
4. Seniors who need significant medical attention	4. Charter or private schools
5. Seniors who need very little medical attention	5. Local grocery stores
6. Seniors with significant mobile constraints	6. Manufacturers of packaged vegetables
7. Seniors who are single but would like a roommate	7. Food banks
8. Seniors who drive	8. Corporate offices that have cafeterias
9. Seniors who want to be able to cook in their apartments	9. People who like to shop at farmers' markets
10. Seniors whose families live far away	10. Local hospitals

From all the potential segments of consumers and customers of your social impact idea, circle the three segments from Exercise 3.1 that you'd like to select as targets and list them in Exercise 3.2.

3 Target Consumers or Customers
1.
2.
3.

Positioning

Finally, let us look at the third step of the STP framework—positioning. Positioning is a term used to describe a product's value in a consumer's mind usually in comparison to competitive products or alternatives. Marketers create *positioning statements* to articulate what they would like this positioning to be. These statements are usually two to three sentences long and have three components—*Target*, *Benefit*, and *Reason to Believe.* Here is a short explanation of each of the components:

- ▶ **Target:** one of your three chosen priority consumer segments
- ▶ **Benefit:** the value or advantage your product or service provides
- ▶ **Reason to Believe:** the credential your product or service has and why a consumer should choose your product over others

Exhibits 3.3 and 3.4 show positioning statements for each target consumer of the senior living center and the indoor vertical farm, with the target, benefits, and reasons to believe highlighted.

EXHIBIT 3.3 Positioning Statements for a Senior Living Center

Senior Living Center Positioning Statements for Each Target Consumer

1. For seniors who are single and want to maintain active social lives, SSLC provides opportunities to live in one or two-bedroom apartments (we help match residents with a roommate if desired) in a complex that offers daily brunch, happy hour, and dinner with multiple activities like yoga, card tournaments, and field trips to develop friendships. Yearly surveys reveal that our residents feel they have never been so active in their entire lives!

2. For married seniors, SSLC provides luxurious "right-sized" apartments which come with a weekly cleaning service. Last year's economic report for the county showed couples on average save 60% in mortgage and home maintenance expenses when living at SSLC.

3. For seniors who need a little medical attention, the Silver Seniors Living Community (SSLC) has licensed nurse practitioners on premises 24 hours a day who can assist residents with routine and ad-hoc medical needs. The nurses go through monthly evaluations not only by the center's leadership, but through anonymous resident evaluations. The SSLC has the highest satisfaction ratings from residents for nurses on staff than any other senior living center in the city!

Key:
| Target Consumer |
| Benefits |
| Reason to Believe |

EXHIBIT 3.4 Positioning Statements for an Indoor Vertical Farm

Indoor Vertical Farm Positioning Statements for Each Target Customer

1. For school districts with 7–10 school campuses, Victory Greens provides nutritious, fresh, and reliable produce to fulfill the government's fruit and vegetable requirements for school cafeterias. School districts that contract with Victory Greens have 50% higher student satisfaction ratings for cafeteria meals than that of schools with other vendors.

2. Victory Greens provides manufacturers of packaged vegetables the freshest produce for freezing since shipments happen in refrigerated trucks with produce still on the vines. Traditional farm deliveries take approximately 1.5 days to arrive at a manufacturing site for packaging, while Victory Greens' truck to freezing time is approximately 20 minutes.

3. Victory Greens provides nutritious, fresh, and reliable produce to local food banks who need to supplement the canned food donations it receives from the community. Year after year, food banks report that the fresh produce is the #1 food item community members appreciate.

Key:
Target Consumer
Benefits
Reason to Believe

Tips for Creating Crisp Benefits and Reasons to Believe

Before crafting the positioning statements for your idea, here is a tip to create benefits that are crisp and compelling. Try to define what your product is and isn't. For example, if you are an organization that raises money for breast cancer and there are other organizations that do something similar, you might specify that your organization focuses solely on funding research (while other organizations fund treatment services). Here are more examples:

- If you are a school uniform provider to low-income families:
  - You *build confidence and self-esteem*, not just give clothes
  - The clothes you give are *free* but have *value*
- If you are an after-school mentoring program:
  - You offer a place to *grow*, not a place to *go*
  - You have a program that is *local* and *customized* to the community, not a national, one-size-fits-all program
  - The program is offered through a *scholarship*, it is not free admission
- If your organization is focused on women's empowerment:
  - You work with domestic violence *survivors*, not victims
  - Your program is *relational*, not transactional

Notice how these very specific word choices and benefits aren't always synonyms or exact opposites. They express nuances.

Now you try it for your product or idea's benefits. Follow this format: Your product is _____ but not _____.

EXERCISE 3.3 Define What Your Product's Benefits *Are* and *Are Not*

Benefits of Your Product or Service
1.
2.
3.

When creating your positioning statements' reasons to believe, try to use data points to make them as compelling as possible. Quantifiable survey results or even qualitative testimonials can accomplish this well.

With this understanding of the target, benefits, and reasons to believe, try to create positioning statements for your three target consumers.

EXERCISE 3.4 Create Positioning Statements

Positioning Statements for Each of Your Product's Target Consumers
1.
2.
3.

By writing these positioning statements, you now have a clear articulation of the value you bring to your consumers' lives. You can use these statements when you are talking to potential consumers, customers, business partners, or donors. If ever you want to expand your product offerings to new consumers, use the STP framework and the exercises in this chapter to ensure the people you want to serve feel special, as though your social impact product or service was created specifically with them in mind.

CONNECTING THE DOTS

After completing the exercises on segmentation, targeting, and positioning, you likely feel stronger about your understanding of your target consumers and the value you bring to their lives. So go back to Chapter 2 and review Exercise 2.1. See if you'd like to add anything to how you describe your target consumers and their problems to solve. Looking forward to Chapters 5–8, you will use this consumer understanding to create a compelling visual identity, website, campaign, and social media strategy.

CHAPTER 4

Research Approach: Testing Your Ideas

After doing the foundational work in Chapters 1, 2, and 3, you are likely getting excited (and perhaps impatient) to start executing your idea. Climate change, gender equality, quality education—these are urgent issues, let's go! But as the sayings go, haste makes waste, go slow to go fast, a stitch in time saves nine…. Pick any adage, the wisdom should be heeded.

Spending time conducting research and testing your idea before you do a full launch is always advised. Just as you wouldn't try a new recipe to take to a dinner party without first testing it on your family and friends, a marketer wouldn't launch a product without researching and testing the idea with its target consumers first. This chapter will cover five steps for a research approach that can help ensure your idea is best set up for a successful launch. It will also point out where you should take extra considerations given your idea is for social impact.

To see the importance of a comprehensive research approach, take a look at what Sun Chips, the snack brand owned by parent company PepsiCo, faced in 2010. The brand was proud to introduce a new packaging innovation that was better for the environment—a 100% compostable package. Compostable packaging, made with plant-based materials, meant the packaging would no longer have to end up in a landfill, it would decompose in the earth through a proper composting process. The company spent significant energy testing the technical components of the packaging while ensuring it still protected the freshness of the chips inside. With confidence in its science, the brand launched the packaging in a big way. It changed the graphics on its bags; one third of its front of pack messaging now had a banner with a claim "World's first 100% compostable bag." All six of its most popular flavors converted their packaging to this new material. A huge media and PR effort was launched to promote it. Though the innovation initially met with a lot of excitement both from consumers and environmental organizations, soon after the launch a problem surfaced. The bag made a very loud crinkling noise when it was handled. It was so loud that a Facebook page was created titled "SORRY BUT I CAN'T HEAR YOU OVER THIS SUN CHIPS BAG." The page was liked by more than 44,000 users. This reaction from consumers prompted the company to return the brand to its original packaging. While the brand had a technically correct social impact idea, not testing the solution first with consumers resulted in some unintended consequences.

The company's research and development team stuck with it though, and after many years of working to optimize the packaging, PepsiCo decided to relaunch the innovation in 2018. This time however, there was much more comprehensive testing. Prior to its relaunch, the packaging was shown to 200 consumers who were asked to pick up the bag, open it up, and see if they noticed anything different about it compared to the regular bag sitting next to it. From these interviews, marketers learned that while consumers did not notice any difference in the crinkling volume of the old versus new packaging, the consumers uncovered two new concerns:

1. There was a slight lack of vibrancy in the colors of the new packaging's graphics.

2. The new packaging was a bit more difficult to open.

This research helped the PepsiCo team address these issues and optimize the bag even further before the new packaging hit stores. And this time PepsiCo launched the improved packaging in Chile, a country whose citizens are very engaged in sustainability. Instead of converting a whole brand's portfolio of flavors with the new packaging, it was introduced in only the regular salted flavor of its brand Lay's Artesanas. It was also only launched in the stores of one retailer, Lider. The limited nature of this pilot helped the company gain confidence in the proposition in a low risk fashion.

Hand in hand with testing the consumer experience, testing that your tone of voice in a campaign lands in the way you intend it to is also vitally important. The issues social impact work addresses are usually emotionally charged and require a heightened level of judgement when creating campaigns around them. In 2017, Facebook's CEO Mark Zuckerberg attempted to showcase features of a new virtual reality tool his company was launching. After a devastating hurricane hit Puerto Rico, while physically at Facebook's offices in California, Zuckerberg appeared in an avatar that livestreamed scenes of the catastrophic damage on the island. While he stated, "My goal here was to show how VR can raise awareness and help us see what's happening in different parts of the world," he was criticized by the public for exploiting the tragic national disaster. His comments were seen as tone deaf and insensitive, and he subsequently released an apology. While stating, "One of the most powerful features of VR is empathy" his comments came off exactly opposite.

In these two examples you see how research and testing can not only save you time and money, it can usually save you from unintended consequences.

In this chapter we will create a research plan for your idea so you can launch it with confidence. Let's begin by reviewing some basic research concepts: primary and secondary research, and quantitative and qualitative data.

- ▶ **Primary Research:** This is custom research conducted especially for your product or idea. Designing and conducting primary research so that it gives you insightful findings is a skill that takes time to develop. Many marketers at large companies have partners in an insights function dedicated to designing and executing research studies. Smaller companies typically hire consultants who have expertise in conducting research. This book will skim the surface of how to conduct primary research and focus more on unique considerations for social impact issues.

- ▶ **Secondary Research:** This is existing research that relates to the issue you are working on. Reviewing secondary research can help you benefit from past successes or failures of those who have tried ideas similar to yours. Reviewing data from research conducted by others can also save you time and money from having to do it yourself.

- **Quantitative Data:** This is numerical data that is usually captured through questions that have a finite set of answer choices. This could include multiple-choice, true or false, or on a scale (e.g. "on a scale of one to ten") type questions. Quantitative data can be expressed in percentages or absolute numbers and can be easily displayed in a graph. Quantitative data can help build credibility in the need for a particular product or service (e.g., "Over 5 million people in country x do not have access to clean drinking water") and show the importance of an issue (e.g., "90% of citizens say a political candidate's stance on climate change is an important factor in who they will vote for").

- **Qualitative Data:** Qualitative data is non-numerical and captures feelings. This type of data is usually gathered through focus groups or in one-on-one interviews (e.g., you might get a quote in an interview like, "When the non-profit helped decorate my first apartment after I came out of homelessness, I felt a sense of dignity and excitement. I felt the community's support as I entered this new chapter in my life.") These types of sentiments cannot be captured in quantitative data points but paint a very compelling picture.

Now that we have reviewed the fundamentals of primary and secondary research, and the nuances between quantitative and qualitative data, let's chat about what makes for a good research approach.

Characteristics of a Good Research Approach for Social Impact Ideas

- **Research is conducted with your target consumers, but also with a wider range of stakeholders.** Most corporate brands focus their research on interviewing their primary target consumers (e.g., "Gen Z young adults who care about living sustainable lifestyles and have purchased x product in the past three months"). However, when creating social impact products or messaging, it is important to also spend some time interviewing a broader set of people who have interest in the issues your product addresses. In the case of compostable snacks packaging, traditionally you would interview your primary consumers, but since you are making environmental claims, you might want to interview someone from The Nature Conservancy, the Alliance to End Plastic Waste, or the Ellen MacArthur Foundation to see how they feel about your product and messaging concepts.

▶ **Research activities include reviewing both primary and secondary data as well as both qualitative and quantitative data.** Your goal is to get a good sense of what people think about your idea, so do not rely on just one survey or one focus group to give you deep, meaningful, and hopefully actionable feedback. Seek feedback from a variety of research avenues.

Now that the importance of research and its various approaches are clear, we will use the five steps below to create your research plan. When balancing the importance of speed to market with the threat of "analysis paralysis" (when too much research leaves you confused on how to move forward), use your judgment.

EXHIBIT 4.1   A 5 Step Research Approach

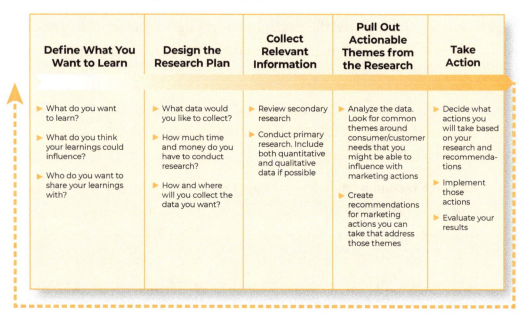

Define What You Want to Learn	Design the Research Plan	Collect Relevant Information	Pull Out Actionable Themes from the Research	Take Action
▶ What do you want to learn? ▶ What do you think your learnings could influence? ▶ Who do you want to share your learnings with?	▶ What data would you like to collect? ▶ How much time and money do you have to conduct research? ▶ How and where will you collect the data you want?	▶ Review secondary research ▶ Conduct primary research. Include both quantitative and qualitative data if possible	▶ Analyze the data. Look for common themes around consumer/customer needs that you might be able to influence with marketing actions ▶ Create recommendations for marketing actions you can take that address those themes	▶ Decide what actions you will take based on your research and recommendations ▶ Implement those actions ▶ Evaluate your results

Step 1: Decide what you want to learn.

The first thing you should do when you start your research is to write down what you hope to learn from it. As you get immersed in reading reports and conducting your research, this list can keep you focused on the data you need to gather. Broadly, these questions can ensure you are taking a comprehensive approach to your research:

1. Can I validate if my target consumers like my idea and approach to bringing it to market?

2. Is there a broader set of key stakeholders outside of my organization who are willing to give me advice and support my idea?

3. Are there any cultural sensitivities I should keep in mind so I don't inadvertently hurt anyone with my idea?

4. What data points do I need to convince my manager/board of directors/ partners that my idea can be successful?

The example in Exhibit 4.2 lays out research objectives and specific questions to explore for an idea for setting up recycling stations in supermarket parking lots.

EXHIBIT 4.2 Research Objectives for an On-Premise Supermarket Recycling Station Idea

Research Objectives

1. I want to get an understanding of what my ***target consumers*** feel about my ideas:
 ► 5 P's:
  ▪ Will shoppers bring their recyclable items (paper, glass, plastic, etc.) when they come to do their grocery shopping?
  ▪ Will shoppers take the time to sort their recyclable items in different bins based on the items' material?
  ▪ Will shoppers expect some type of compensation (cash or coupons?) or will they participate in recycling without expectation of a reward?

- ► 3 C's:
    - ▪ Are there organizations I could collaborate with on this idea?
- ► STP:
    - ▪ Will shoppers find the recycling station valuable? Will they see it as convenient or would they prefer a different recycling system?

2. Given my idea has the potential to impact **a broader system of stakeholders**, I will seek to get input on my social impact idea from these stakeholders outside of my organization:
    - ► Leaders who run existing recycling programs in the city
    - ► Organizers of similar programs in other cities—can they share their learnings with our team?
    - ► Supermarket managers
    - ► Partners who are good at measurement and auditing—I'm hoping they can share ways we might measure the success of this idea

3. I want to understand if there are **cultural sensitivities** to keep in mind given the people and places I want to positively impact with my idea. These are the thought leaders in the social impact space I'm working in that I will seek advice from:
    - ► Environmental activists
    - ► Professors of environmental science

4. I want to keep in mind these key decision makers I need to influence and the data points they care about:
    - ► My board of directors care about how many kilograms of recyclables we'll be able to collect through this program.
    - ► Supermarket managers I want to partner with care about if this program will drive increased foot traffic to their stores.

(Note: A recycling program like this exists in Chile. It is named Puntos Limpio and is run by an organization called TriCiclos.)

Now use the template in Exercise 4.1 to write out questions you'd like to explore in your research.

EXERCISE 4.1 Outline Research Objectives for Testing Your Idea

1. I want to get an understanding of what my **target consumers** feel about my ideas:

   ▶ 5 P's:

   ▶ 3 C's:

   ▶ STP:

2. Given my idea has the potential to impact **a broader system of stakeholders**, I will seek to get input on my social impact idea from these stakeholders outside of my organization:

   ▶

   ▶

   ▶

3. I want to understand if there are any **cultural sensitivities** to keep in mind given the people and places I want to positively impact with my idea. These are the thought leaders in the social impact space I'm working in that I will seek input from:

   ▶

   ▶

   ▶

4. I want to keep in mind these key decision makers I need to influence and the data points they care about:

   ▶

   ▶

   ▶

Step 2: Design your research plan.

It's sneaky, but we have three sub-steps under Step 2:

2a) Determine the data you want to collect.

2b) Define your research constraints.

2c) Determine where and how you are going to collect the data you want.

2a) To determine what data you want to collect during your research, simply think about the knowledge you need to successfully execute and validate your idea.

EXHIBIT 4.3 Data Needs for an On-Premise Supermarket Recycling Station Idea

Data to Gather via Research
▶ How many kilograms of recyclable material do we think we'll collect each week?
▶ With what frequency do we need to empty out our recycling station and transport the collected material?
▶ Are there any time periods during the day where we can expect higher or lower traffic? What type of staffing needs are required to handle this level of activity?
▶ Will people think more favorably of the supermarket if it has this recycling station on-premise?
▶ Do people visit the supermarket more frequently when it has this recycling station?

Write down the data you want to collect in your research in Exercise 4.2.

EXERCISE 4.2 Data Needed to Execute and Validate Your Social Impact Idea

Data to Gather via Research
▶
▶
▶
▶
▶

2b) You likely do not have unlimited time, money, or people to help you with your research. Therefore, it's prudent to think realistically about what data you can gather with the resources you have. Outline your research constraints by thinking about:

▶ **Time:** When do you need to finish fielding and analyzing your research? If the research results suggest that you should tweak your 5 P's, 3 C's, or your positionings, do you have time built in to make these changes before your launch?

▶ **Money:** Do you have a budget for primary research? For example, if you want to distribute a survey or conduct a focus group, you might incentivize or reward participants for their time with small gift cards. Secondary research on social impact issues is typically shared freely, but you might need a budget for this as well.

▶ **People:** Do you have staff or volunteers who can help you field primary research and collect and read through secondary research?

► **Unique cultural or environmental considerations:** If you are doing the research in an ethnically diverse neighborhood, do you need to do surveys, interviews, and focus groups in multiple languages? Do you need a translator? Could inclement weather affect your schedule?

EXHIBIT 4.4 Examples of Research Constraints

Research Constraints
1. I only have 4 weeks to conduct and analyze the research.
2. I need to write our surveys and conduct our focus groups in both Spanish and English.
3. I can only get time with my target audience during lunch hours so I should budget getting sandwiches and drinks for the focus group participants.

What constraints do you have to test your idea? Capture them in Exercise 4.3.

EXERCISE 4.3   Define Your Research Constraints

Research Constraints
1.
2.
3.

2c) When determining where and how you are going to collect data, you might want to start identifying secondary data sources first. See what research questions you can get answered before starting your custom primary research. Exhibit 4.5 has suggestions of where you can find secondary data.

EXHIBIT 4.5   Secondary Research Sources

Secondary Research Sources
▸ The United Nations Sustainable Development Goals' website has information on 17 social impact areas that countries around the world have aligned on to address: https://sustainabledevelopment.un.org/sdgs
▸ Government databases (like the U.S. Census) have demographic information https://www.census.gov/
▸ Industry and trade organizations might have reports related to your work that are free to access.
▸ Reports from research your organization has conducted in the past might contain baseline data from where you might be able to pick up with new research.
▸ Organizations that do similar work to yours might have reports they are willing to share given the collaborative nature of social impact work.

Take time to brainstorm secondary research sources you might be able to tap into and record them in Exercise 4.4.

EXERCISE 4.4 List Secondary Research Sources Containing Data Pertinent to Your Idea

Secondary Research Sources
▶
▶
▶

Now think about how you might conduct primary research. Custom research that provides meaningful and actionable data requires quite a bit of thought and planning. Ideally, you'd want to gather enough data so it is statistically significant (which in simple terms means you've surveyed enough people that results from your interviewees reflect how the entire population you are trying to reach would respond). Realistically though, you'll likely have research constraints that might limit how many people you can talk to. Try to interview as many people as possible until you start seeing themes in people's responses.

Here are a few ways to do primary research:

Left: © Antonio Guillem/Shutterstock.com; middle: © Monkey Business Images/Shutterstock.com; right: © McLittle Stock/Shutterstock.com

EXHIBIT 4.6 · Methods of Conducting Primary Research

Primary Research Approaches
▸ One-on-one interviews (you can conduct these in-person or through online survey tools like SurveyMonkey, Google Forms, or Facebook Poll)
▸ Focus groups
▸ Shopalongs (where you go shopping with someone to watch their in-store purchase behavior)
▸ Observation (where you note how someone behaves in a certain environment with and/or without your product)

Exhibit 4.7 provides an example of how you might approach primary research for the on-premise supermarket recycling station idea.

EXHIBIT 4.7 Primary Research Approach for On-Premise Supermarket Recycling Station Idea

Primary Research Approaches
▶ One-on-one digital and printed surveys with shoppers entering and exiting the supermarket. These surveys will include both quantitative and qualitative questions.
▶ Focus groups of supermarket store managers, three to five managers will be interviewed at a time
▶ One-on-one interviews with people who have experience operating recycling programs
▶ One-on-one interviews with environmental activists and professors of environmental science

Think about how you want to approach primary research for your idea and capture your thoughts in Exercise 4.5.

EXERCISE 4.5 List How You'd Like to Conduct Primary Research

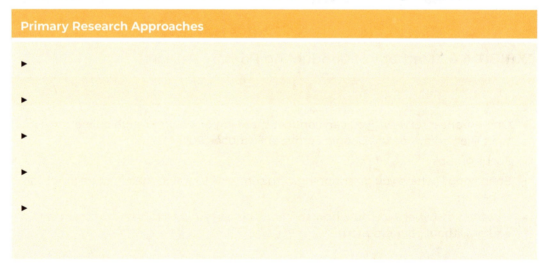

Primary Research Approaches
▶
▶
▶
▶
▶

Step 3: Collect relevant data.

In this data collection phase, start by taking note of the key learnings you gather from secondary data sources. Then move on to conducting your primary research. When conducting primary research, try to get as close to your target consumers as possible. This means visiting the neighborhoods they live in and interviewing them where they work and where they live. This means more in-person interviews and fewer online surveys, which is natural for our nonprofit leaders who spend time doing grassroots level work. Their offices are usually located right in the neighborhoods they serve. But for our corporate marketers, who work in beautiful corporate offices, this type of immersion requires a shift in mindset and behavior.

Bryan Stevenson, a lawyer, criminal justice activist, and the founder of the Equal Justice Initiative, talks about the power of proximity, of getting close to a cause. He says in an address to Harvard's Kennedy School students posted online on January 31, 2019,

> *We think we can change the world by staying just on Harvard's campus, by staying in places of power and privilege, staying just in our elected offices. If we care about injustice, if we care about inequality, if we care about poverty, if we care about disability, if we care about addiction and dependency, we're going to have to get close enough to those who are poor and excluded and neglected, addicted and dependent, to understand the nature of that problem.*
>
> Excerpt from a speech delivered to Harvard's Kennedy School students by Bryan Stevenson, posted on YouTube.

So corporate marketers, challenge yourselves to spend time in the neighborhoods and with the people you want your social impact marketing campaigns to serve. And students, challenge yourselves to get off campus as well. Volunteer at the food banks and homeless shelters. But also remember, if you are going to a dicey part of town, go with a group of adults, go during daylight hours, and be aware of your surroundings. Always stay safe.

With this approach in mind, prepare your set of interview questions. Include both quantitative and qualitative questions. To see an example of a mix of questions and formats, check out Exhibit 4.8. We will now move away from the recycling station idea to an idea focused on helping individuals transitioning out of the prison system. New nonprofits are forming to support this population with tools and services that can help them with re-entry into civil society.

EXHIBIT 4.8 Research Questions to Ask of Individuals Who Have Transitioned out of the Prison System and Back into Civil Society

Survey Questions

- ▸ Quantitative questions:
  - ▪ True or False: I had a support system to help me transition when I got home.
  - ▪ Multiple-Choice: Which of these things could you have used help with:
    - ◊ Getting a driver's license
    - ◊ Interview preparation
    - ◊ Financial literacy
  - ▪ Yes or No: Would you have liked help creating a resume?

- ▸ Qualitative questions:
  - ▪ What industry or type of work would you like to do?
  - ▪ Do you have any physical conditions we should keep in mind as we help you find different employment opportunities?

Focus Group and One-on-One Interview Questions

- ▸ Qualitative questions:
  - ▪ What were you most worried about for your transition out of prison?
  - ▪ Were you aware of any resources that could have helped you in your transition?
  - ▪ What kind of tools do you think would be helpful for people returning home?
  - ▪ Is there anything you'd like to share with us about your experience?

Use the template in Exercise 4.6 to draft questions for your primary research. When conducting your actual research though, print out the questions in a formal survey format (or use a digital tool to do the same).

EXERCISE 4.6 Draft Your Research Questions

▶ Quantitative questions:

-

-

-

▶ Qualitative questions:

-

-

-

Focus Group and One-on-One Interview Questions

▶ Qualitative questions:

-

-

In the first few interviews and surveys you conduct, notice how long it takes for your interviewees to answer your questions. Did the interviews feel too long or too short? Did people get tired of answering your questions or did they want to give you more of their thoughts and feedback? Did people give meaningful answers to the questions you asked? Or would it have been better if you asked the questions in a different way? Adjust your questions accordingly.

Step 4: Pull out Actionable Themes from the Research

After collecting your primary and secondary data, start compiling notes on what you found most interesting. Analyze the data to see if you can identify common themes. Graph your quantitative data and see what stands out—is there a question that a significant number of people answered in a certain way? In your qualitative data, are there sentiments that frequently emerged? Did you learn anything that surprised you and make you want to reconsider some of your 5 P's, 3 C's, and positioning statements?

Based on your key findings, think through what actions you could take to address each one of them. Refer to Exhibit 4.9 to see how this analysis can be organized in a chart. In the example, we see how an organization that brings yoga classes to an underserved community could organize their key findings and recommendations by its target consumers—parents, kids, and senior citizens.

EXHIBIT 4.9 Key Findings and Recommendations for a Yoga Program Designed for an Underserved Community

Research Findings and Recommendations

Parents

Key Finding 1: The number 1 reason that parents say will prevent them from taking a yoga class is the worry about finding childcare for their kids.	Recommendation 1: Offer a kids' yoga class at the same time in an adjacent room to the parents' yoga class.
Key Finding 2: 90% of parents in under-resourced communities rely on government food subsidies, and thus do not have a lot of disposable income to spend on themselves.	Recommendation 2: Seek donors to cover the costs of classes so that they can be offered for free or minimal cost.
Key Finding 3: 75% of parents are not convinced there are mental and physical health benefits of yoga.	Recommendation 3: Enlist the help of community influencers like church/mosque/temple leaders, teachers, and recreation center directors to help distribute information on the benefits of yoga.

Kids

Key Finding 1: Research shows that kids between the ages of 4–8 have attention spans of 30 minutes for an activity, while kids ages 9–18 can hold their attention for up to 1 hour.	Recommendation 1: Create two program lengths—30 minutes and 60 minutes for the different age groups. Have activities for the younger kids after their yoga class to occupy them until their parents are done with the adult class.
Key Finding 2: Schools that incorporate yoga into their curriculum claim their students report 40% less anxiety and they have 25% less disciplinary issues than schools that don't have yoga classes.	Recommendation 2: Approach principals and physical education teachers with this research to discuss ways to incorporate yoga into their curriculum, recess, after-school, or physical education programs.
Key Finding 3: Students who do yoga regularly perform 60% better on standardized tests.	Recommendation 3: Speak at teacher training seminars to educate teachers on the benefits of yoga and how to teach it in their classrooms.

Seniors

Key Finding 1: In focus groups, seniors told us they enjoy more meditation and breathing exercises over doing a sequence of poses.	Recommendation 1: Incorporate more minutes of breathing exercises and meditation into each yoga class.
Key Finding 2: Seniors enjoyed guided meditations over sitting silently with music.	Recommendation 2: Provide guided meditations in senior citizen classes.
Key Finding 3: Seniors with joint pain found some poses difficult and, thus, were hesitant to continue classes.	Recommendation 3: Offer cushions, pillows, and thick blankets to sit on for comfort during senior classes. During class emphasize different variations for poses that could be difficult.

Analyze data from both your primary and secondary research and try to pull out key themes. In Exercise 4.7 develop recommendations for marketing actions that address these key themes, and organize your notes by your target consumers.

EXERCISE 4.7 Succinctly Summarize Your Key Findings and Develop Corresponding Recommendations

Research Findings and Recommendations	
Target Consumer Group 1	
Key Finding 1:	Recommendation 1:
Key Finding 2:	Recommendation 2:
Key Finding 3:	Recommendation 3:

Target Consumer Group 2

Key Finding 1:	Recommendation 1:
Key Finding 2:	Recommendation 2:
Key Finding 3:	Recommendation 3:

Target Consumer Group 3

Key Finding 1:	Recommendation 1:
Key Finding 2:	Recommendation 2:
Key Finding 3:	Recommendation 3:

Step 5: Take Action

The final step of your research approach is to actually launch your idea into the world. To do so, you will have the help of the exercises in the next 5 chapters of this book. Constantly monitor how consumers react to your marketing activations, look for key themes, and develop recommendations for how to keep serving your targets; research should never be "finished."

CONNECTING THE DOTS

Based on the research you conducted and analyzed through the exercises in this chapter, reflect on whether or not your findings validate and give you confidence in the plans you laid out in Chapters 1, 2, and 3. Make any modifications necessary and proceed to Part 2 of this book.

PART 2
ACT

These chapters in Part 2 will help you bring to life what you planned for in Part 1. You will learn how to engage your target consumers and broader stakeholders by creating a visual identity, a website, campaigns, social media and a public relations strategy for your brand. We will tackle these elements one chapter at a time.

CHAPTER 5

Visual Identity: How to Build Brand Recognition

When you want to make a good first impression, you probably dress up. You make sure your outfit is coordinated and matches your personality. You hope that with one glance, people understand what you're about (or that they'll be intrigued to learn more). In a similar sense, creating a visual identity is how you dress up an idea or a brand. A brand's visual identity—it's logo, colors, fonts, images it uses—triggers mental associations about what a brand stands for.

When starting an organization, many hope to create a logo that's as globally recognizable as Nike or McDonald's. It's great to have this ambition, just know that it has taken decades of significant marketing investments to make these logos so iconic. Rest assured, this chapter will take you through the steps of how to create a logo and visual identity that will put you on this path.

Brand recognition is a strong result of a great visual identity, but at a deeper level, it can also help convey your brand's values. For example, many people easily recognize retailer Target's red and white color scheme and its "bullseye" logo. Immediately people have mental associations with the brand as a place you can turn to for everyday items, albeit with an added extra bit of style and design. In 2017 Target's Cat & Jack clothing line launched its adaptive apparel collection for kids living with disabilities. Its advertising highlighted the clothing's special features, such as side and back zip closures, hidden openings for abdominal access, and tag-less options that are sensory-friendly. At the photo shoot for the line, kids with disabilities were brought in to be the models for the clothes. In an industry that conventionally used a standard type of model, this was quite remarkable. When Target takes effort to include models of all shapes, sizes, ethnicities, and physical abilities in its advertisements, it cues that it is a brand that values diversity and is truly trying to design for everyone in mind.

Target Cat and Jack Adaptive Line. Watch a behind the scenes look here: https://corporate.target.com/videos/corporate-responsibility/ 2018-cr-marketing/cr-cat-and-jack-2018.

This is the power of a visual identity. The visual identity *shows* your audience what your brand stands for, without you having to *tell* them. Let's now discuss what constitutes a strong visual identity so we can keep this in mind as we go through the steps of creating one for your social impact organization.

Characteristics of a Strong Visual Identity

► **The logo is easily recognizable both from a distance and in small spaces.** Your logo could be printed on billboards that people see when driving on a highway, and it can also be on a thumbnail image of your brand's social media handles. Therefore, fancy lettering and complicated styling could make text in a logo hard to read.

► **The visual identity is used frequently and consistently on all marketing touchpoints.** This effort creates recognition and familiarity with your brand. (In addition to creating positive sentiments, building recognition is an important element of building brand equity. Recall that building brand equity is one of the core goals of marketing.) Your logo and other elements of your visual identity should likely be on your product, on your organization's website, on the social media images you post, the posters, print ads, and videos you create, and even on the letterhead and signature you use if you are sending a letter or an email. The more places people see your logo, the more they will come to recognize it.

► **Elements of the visual identity are unique and symbolic.** A challenge that many nonprofits face in building brand recognition comes from using symbols in their logos that could be interchangeable with other organizations. Many use images of trees in their logos to symbolize growth, many use open palms to represent giving, and many use shaking hands to symbolize partnership. While these are common practices of nonprofits, they are not unique. When creating the visual identity for your brand, try choosing symbols that represent the unique nature of your social impact work. An example of a brand that has done this well is the Olympic Games, whose "ultimate goal of cultivating people and world peace through sports" has a logo of interlaced rings of multiple colors. These symbolize "the union of the five continents and the meeting of athletes from throughout the world at the Olympic Games." (International Olympic Committee, n.d.) The logo is simple yet meaningful; it represents only what the Olympics can do.

After reviewing these best practices, let's now start working on creating your brand's visual identity. You can tackle this effort yourself through the following steps, or you could do the exercises with the help of someone with professional design experience. You'll get guidance on working with professional designers later in the chapter, too.

Step 1: Choose a color palette.

A fairly easy place to start when creating a visual identity is choosing a color palette. Certain colors have meanings given to them by culture, and several colors have come to represent specific social impact causes like:

► Red —→ Heart health

► Purple —→ Domestic violence, pancreatic cancer

► Pink —→ Breast cancer

► Green —→ Environmentalism

From left to right: © koblizeek/Shutterstock.com, © scoutori/Shutterstock.com,
© Albert999/Shutterstock.com, © DomeLifeThibaan/Shutterstock.com

While it isn't required that your brand's color palette reflect these common associations, your brand could benefit from the mental associations consumers already have with these colors.

Moreover, colors can drive certain human reactions. Blue is known to have a calming effect. Red is fiery and energetic and represents good luck in certain cultures. Black signifies premium and luxury in many societies. White can signify purity. Yellow is known to drive appetite appeal. (Have you noticed how both Lay's Classic potato chips and McDonald's have iconic yellow logos?) Brown, green, and earthy tones usually signify natural or organic products; and so on.

Reflecting on the colors your competitors and collaborators are using is also a good practice. You could mimic them to benefit from the equity they've built with their color palette, or you could adopt a starkly different color palette in an effort to stand out. Neither way is right or wrong, you should just be mindful of the choice you are making.

Attempt to fill out the questions in Exercise 5.1 to start defining a color palette for your visual identity.

EXERCISE 5.1 Analyze Color Options for Your Brand's Visual Identity

Colors in My Brand's Visual Identity
These are colors associated with my social impact cause area:
How I want my target consumers to feel when they use my product (e.g. calm, energized, patriotic?):
Colors that drive those feelings:
Colors my competitors and collaborators are using:
Why I want my brand colors to be similar to or different than theirs:

Step 2: Identify symbols that can represent your product or service.

Certain symbols have the power to reveal immediately to a consumer what a social impact organization's mission is. For example, an image of a house in a nonprofit's logo could symbolize its mission to provide shelter for those experiencing homelessness. Elements and colors of a country's flag could symbolize a mission to provide services for veterans. Images of books or of a graduation cap could symbolize a mission focused on education. Here are additional symbols that have come to represent social impact missions and causes:

- ▶ Puzzle pieces ⟶ Autism awareness
- ▶ Rainbows ⟶ LGBTQ+ rights
- ▶ Infinity loop ⟶ Recycling and a circular economy
- ▶ Trees ⟶ Personal growth, environmental advocacy

From left to right: © NEGOVURA/Shutterstock.com, © Ink Drop/Shutterstock.com, © SoRad/Shutterstock.com, © KreativKolors/Shutterstock.com

Think through symbols that could represent your services and capture them in Exercise 5.2. Remember per the guidance above, try to pick symbols that represent what your organization uniquely does.

EXERCISE 5.2   Choose Symbols for Your Brand's Visual Identity

Symbols Important to My Brand's Visual Identity
Symbols and images that represent the mission of my social impact idea:
Symbols my collaborators and competitors are using: (draw or list them below)

Step 3: Select a font that represents your brand's personality.

Fonts, in addition to colors and symbols, play a key role in a brand's visual identity. A font is essentially the style of letters you use to communicate your brand's personality. You might want a font for your logo and an additional font to use on your website and printed materials. Keep these elements in mind when choosing fonts:

▶ Serif fonts ⟶ have decorative marks on the edges of their letters. These fonts are considered elegant and classic. Times New Roman is an example of a serif font.

▶ Sans serif fonts ⟶ do not have a serif. These fonts are considered modern, clean and friendly. Arial is an example of a sans serif font.

- ▶ Rounded fonts ⟶ appear fun and playful
- ▶ Script fonts ⟶ are decorative in nature and are better used for logos and statements than long form text

Complete Exercise 5.3 to capture your thoughts about the fonts you'd like to consider.

EXERCISE 5.3   Brainstorm Font Styles for Your Brand's Visual Identity

Fonts for My Brand's Visual Identity
The personality I want my fonts to convey (e.g. established, formal, serious, approachable, friendly, playful):
Images of fonts I'd like to consider for my logo:
For the text on my website and printed materials, I think a _____ (serif or a sans serif) font best reflects my brand's personality.

Step 4: Design the logo and create a style guide.

Now that you've done the preparatory work of identifying meaningful colors, symbols, and fonts, it is time to design the logo and create a style guide for your brand's visual identity. Here is when you might seek out professional designers to help you. While marketers are creative and analytical, many are not trained in graphic design. Marketers at large corporations often work through Steps 1–3 and then typically seek help from in-house designers at their companies, or they seek help from a professional design firm outside their company. If you are not savvy with design tools, you might consider these options to actually create your designs:

▶ Search for an online logo generator/creator.

▶ Seek help from volunteer designers. (TaprootFoundation.org and Voly.org are organizations that help connect volunteers with nonprofits. You can post your design project on their sites and see if any volunteer designers are available.)

▶ Hire a professional graphic designer. (You can search for freelance designers online or ask your colleagues and friends for recommendations of people they have worked with in the past.)

Designers know how to use technical tools like Adobe Illustrator to create logos in high resolution file formats. High resolution files work well to maintain design ratios when you have to adjust the size of a logo to fit different marketing collateral (like websites, T-shirts, banners, business cards, etc.)

If you will be asking someone for help, it's a good idea to put all your thoughts into what marketing professionals call a ***design brief***. Review Exhibit 5.1 for an example of a logo design brief.

EXHIBIT 5.1   Sample Logo Brief

Dallas Heroes Project
Logo Design Brief

Briefing Date: May 15, 2019
Client: Dallas Heroes Project
Designer: Trevor Ezaki

Objective:
Create a refreshed logo and a style guide (fonts, colors) for the Dallas Heroes Project's visual identity.

Problem to Solve:
The current logo was a placeholder while the organization got off the ground. It is quite generic and does not represent the organization's mission.

Current logo:

Dallas Heroes Project's Background and Mission:
There is so much good being done in Dallas, so many non-profits exist, but the majority of us don't know about them. We can participate in a 5k or write a check, but many of us want to do more, and learn about more opportunities to donate to causes that we connect with. Dallas Heroes Project aims to bring forward the great non-profits of this city to connect them with people who want to get involved. In this age of turmoil and terrorism, DHP exists to shed light on positive change and action.

Mission: The Dallas Heroes project celebrates local heroes, educating citizens on critical issues facing the city, and enables citizens to take social action to make a positive impact in the Dallas Metroplex.

For reference, here are some of the organization's current social sites:
www.dallasheroesproject.org
www.facebook.com/dallasheroesproject
https://www.instagram.com/dallasheroesproject/

1

Target Audience:

Dallas Heroes Project has 3 main target audiences:

- Students – this group needs community service hours for high school and college requirements. They can primarily volunteer *time*.
- Working Professionals – this group (Millennials and Gen X'ers) like to be hands-on in their giving. They want to donate their time in a professional capacity (helping with strategic plans, marketing, financial planning, technology, human resources, etc. They do not like spending money on galas as they see the expense for that is better spent on a nonprofit's programming.
- Retirees – this group is high on time and *money* to donate. They enjoy galas as its an opportunity to socialize and network.

Design Considerations:

- A heart might be a nice symbol to explore given we are designing for a nonprofit organization
- The DHP leadership is hoping the brand looks "professional, local, and warm."

Deliverables:

- New logo – in PNG and JPEG formats to be used vertically, horizontally, in black and white, 2 color, and 4 color options
- Style guide – with font names and brand colors

Timeline:

- May 21: Trevor to share Round 1 designs
- May 25: DHP to provide consolidated feedback to Trevor
- May 31: Trevor to share Round 2 designs
- June 6: DHP to provide consolidated feedback
- June 13th: Trevor to deliver final logo and style guide

2

Complete Exercise 5.4 to create a logo brief for your social impact product or idea.

EXERCISE 5.4   Write a Logo Design Brief

Organization Name
Logo Design Brief

Briefing Date:

Client:

Designer:

Objective:

Problem to Solve:

Organization's Background, Mission, and Social Assets:
- Background:
- Mission:
- Website and social media sites (if available):

Target Audience:

Design Considerations:
- Colors that should be considered:
- Symbols that reflect the mission of the organization:
- Font styles that reflect the personality of the organization:

Deliverables:
- New logo with vertical and horizontal formats.
  - Create logos with black & white, 2-color and 4-color options.
  - Files should be submitted in .ai, .png, and .jpeg formats.
- Style guide with font names and brand colors

Timeline:

General Timeline for Working with Designers and Creative Agency Partners

Usually, if a logo design brief is crisp and detailed, it takes two to three rounds of creative iterations to land on a logo. After sharing the brief with your designer, expect about two weeks for him or her to come up with some initial sketches of design territories. Review these sketches together in person, over the phone, or on a video chat so you can chat live and understand the designer's thought process behind each of the sketches. Ask the designer if you can provide feedback after two to three days. This will enable you to sit with the sketches for a few days and get feedback on them from your colleagues, target consumers, and broader stakeholders. Then meet with the designer again to discuss the collective feedback live. Explain why you liked or didn't like certain elements so the next iteration of designs can reflect that thinking. Always have feedback discussions live because nuances, especially on things that are creative in nature, get lost in email. After the live conversation, however, you can use email to recap the discussion so that both parties are clear and don't forget the feedback.

Then expect one week for the designer to edit the sketches and come back to you with about three to five designs that now include color. Repeat the process of sitting with the designs for a few days, share them with your stakeholders, and then provide consolidated feedback to the designer live. At this stage, you should be getting close to a logo design you like.

The designer will likely take one more week to make more edits and then share what's likely to be a final design. If you like it, the designer will finalize the logo and send it back to you in various formats—jpeg, png, svg and ai files. The designer can also create versions of your logo that work well in horizontal or vertical spaces. He or she can also send versions that work in full color, just two colors, and in black-and-white. (You want these options because due to budgetary constraints, sometimes you might choose to print in black and white or in 2-colors over the most expensive full 4-color option.)

Exhibit 5.2 contains an example of iterations within a logo design process.

EXHIBIT 5.2 Logo Design Iterations and Final Style Guide for Dallas Heroes Project, an Organization That Helps Nonprofits with Marketing

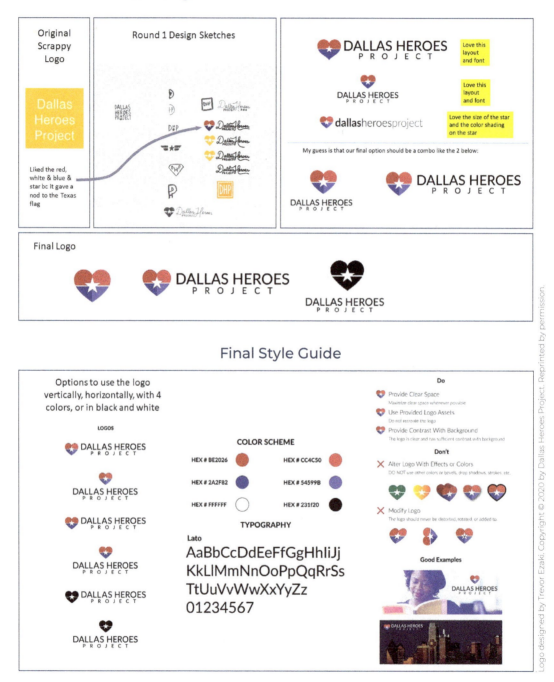

The style guide can be a place to explain additional elements of a brand's visual identity. For example, Target could include notes about how people of all ethnicities, sizes, and physical abilities should be highlighted in their ads.

Now here are some tips on how to provide constructive and efficient feedback during the design process:

Your Mindset

When communicating with your designer, take the approach of sharing your feedback with kindness. Designers are creatives, and creativity requires vulnerability. Imagine how you would feel if someone said, "I hate these designs. They are horrible and ugly and don't work at all for my product." Instead, try starting with appreciation and then address changes you'd like to see in a constructive manner. You could say,

- ▸ "I like the variety of options you've shown here. This is helping me to see that we should try to create a design that is more playful/serious/elegant/organic looking/etc."

- ▸ "I like the colors you've chosen, but can we try to go lighter/darker with these elements?"

- ▸ "On the fonts, I'm not quite sure we're hitting the right tone yet. I like a few of them that look like the right balance of approachable and professional— can we look at a few more options like these?"

- ▸ "Instead of a graduation cap, can we try using a stack of books to symbolize our work?"

Understand that marketers and designers need each other and can be great partners. Marketers are experts in what their brand stands for and who it serves. Designers have the expertise to bring those elements to life visually.

Your Tone

When sharing feedback, if there's a design you like a lot, feel free to express that. "Wow this looks fantastic! I love the way you've brought our idea to life!"

If you don't like the designs, try to maintain a thankful, professional, and objective tone. You can say, "Thank you for sketching those out. That's helped me visualize how my brief comes to life. I might need to edit the brief after seeing this," or "Let's make edits to certain elements to reflect our mission a bit more."

Your Feedback

▸ Be as straightforward as possible in describing what you like and what doesn't feel "on brand" yet. Like you, the designer doesn't want to go through 100 iterations of designs, so be clear and direct (while being kind).

▸ Be straightforward but not too prescriptive. If there's a small, specific edit needed, be clear about that. You can ask for specific changes such as, "We have to swap out red for orange" or "We need to use an (R) mark instead of a (TM) mark." But if you're not feeling good about a logo try not to say, "Increase this element by 5 millimeters, decrease this element by 2 millimeters and try adding a heart or a star." This is too prescriptive and might limit a designer's creativity. Instead try, "Let's figure out how we can better express our organization's personality." Providing this type of constructive feedback takes skill and practice.

▸ Provide consolidated feedback from your team through one person. The consolidated feedback should synthesize the opinions of all stakeholders and be presented with one point of view to the designer. If the designer receives multiple emails from different people within an organization, it can create confusion and can lead to endless rounds of feedback.

Once you've aligned to your logo, symbols, and fonts, your designer can help you organize these elements into a style guide. This example shows pages of New York University's Stern School of Business's logo and visual identity style guide:

NYU | STERN   Primary and Secondary Logos

PRIMARY USE LOGO

All versions of the logo include the institutional mark (torch in the box) and:
- Align the NYU type with the school name, separated by a thin vertical rule
- Should be reproduced in purple and black whenever possible (NYU Violet is PMS 2597 for print, #57068C for digital)
- Within the logo, Stern and the rule should never be purple
- Can appear as black-only when color is not available, or as white when used over a dark background

NYU | STERN   **NYU | STERN**
NYU | STERN   **NYU | STERN**

APPROVED LAYOUTS
SECONDARY LOGO VERSIONS

NYU | LEONARD N. STERN SCHOOL OF BUSINESS   **NYU | LEONARD N. STERN SCHOOL OF BUSINESS**

NYU | LEONARD N. STERN SCHOOL OF BUSINESS   **NYU | LEONARD N. STERN SCHOOL OF BUSINESS**

PRIMARY VERSION:
The primary version of the logo
- Uses the school's common shorthand name, "NYU Stern"
- Is a strong graphical mark
- Is flexible
- Is easily recognized at a distance or in small sizes

SECONDARY VERSIONS:
Secondary versions of the logo
- Contain the expanded school name
- Provide options for vertical stacked layouts

The logo is provided as one piece of art and may not be modified in any way. Do not use another font in place of Gotham in the logo.

SECONDARY LAYOUTS STACKED:

NYU   **NYU**   **NYU**
STERN   **STERN**   **STERN**
                                  OR BLACK BACKGROUND

NYU   **NYU**   **NYU**
**STERN SCHOOL   **STERN SCHOOL   **STERN SCHOOL
OF BUSINESS**   OF BUSINESS**   OF BUSINESS**
                                  OR BLACK BACKGROUND

5

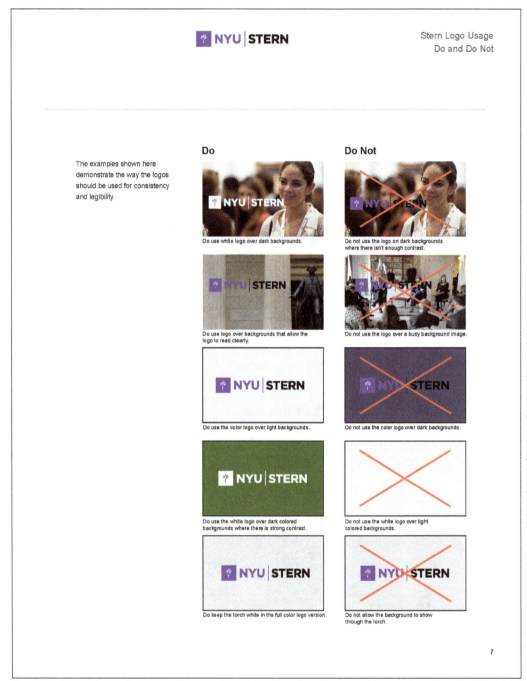

NYU | STERN

The examples shown here demonstrate the way the logos should be used for consistency and legibility.

Do

Do Not

Do use white logo over dark backgrounds.

Do not use the logo on dark backgrounds where there isn't enough contrast.

Do use logo over backgrounds that allow the logo to read clearly.

Do not use the logo over a busy background image.

Do use the color logo over light backgrounds.

Do not use the color logo over dark backgrounds.

Do use the white logo over dark colored backgrounds where there is strong contrast.

Do not use the white logo over light colored backgrounds.

Do keep the torch white in the full color logo version.

Do not allow the background to show through the torch.

7

Primary Color Palette

The color palette is designed to create a consistent and recognizable visual brand for the institution.

These colors are used on the Stern website and may be used in print materials.

Use PMS or CMYK color definitions for print, and RGB or HEX color definitions for digital.

PMS 2597 C
CMYK: 85-100-0-0
RGB: 82-46-145
HEX: 572C86

PMS Cool Gray 11 U
CMYK: 0-2-0-68
RGB: 113-112-115
HEX: 717073

White
CMYK: 0-0-0-0
RGB: 255-255-255
HEX: FFFFFF

Rich Black
CMYK: 40-40-40-100
RGB:
HEX:

PMS Cool Gray 6 U
CMYK: 37-30-29-0
RGB: 166-166-168
HEX: A3A5A8

Secondary Color Palette

PMS 2567 U
CMYK: 24-30-0-0
RGB: 190-161-204
HEX: C09ED9

PMS Cool Gray 1 U
CMYK: 10-7-8-0
RGB: 227-227-227
HEX: E3E3E3

PMS 426
CMYK: 73-6-65-80
RGB: 21-21-21
HEX: 353535

PMS Cool Gray 7
CMYK: 43-35-35-1
RGB: 153-153-153
HEX: 999999

Tertiary Color Palette for Digital

The tertiary color palette is used selectively for digital.

RGB: 126-224-252
HEX: fee0fc

RGB: 254-232-0
HEX: fee800

RGB: 62-14-132
HEX: 7e0e84

12

Do not use another font in place
of Gotham Black and Gotham
Black Italic in the tagline.

For MS Word documents and
MS Powerpoint presentations,
Arial Black and Arial Black Italic
may be used (except for in the
Stern logo).

You may purchase an individual
or group license of the Gotham
font from typography.com.

TAGLINE TYPEFACE:

Gotham Black

ABCDEFGHIJKLMNOPQRSTUVQXYZ
abcdefghijklmnopqrstuvwxyz
1234567890{}:;,.'

Gotham Black Italic

ABCDEFGHIJKLMNOPQRSTUVQXYZ
abcdefghijklmnopqrstuvwxyz
1234567890{}:;,.'

WEB/MICROSOFT TEMPLATE TYPEFACE:

Arial Regular

ABCDEFGHIJKLMNOPQRSTUVQXYZ
abcdefghijklmnopqrstuvwxyz
1234567890{}:;,.'

Arial Italic

ABCDEFGHIJKLMNOPQRSTUVQXYZ
abcdefghijklmnopqrstuvwxyz
1234567890{}:;,.'

Arial Bold

ABCDEFGHIJKLMNOPQRSTUVQXYZ
abcdefghijklmnopqrstuvwxyz
1234567890{}:;,.'

TAGLINE TYPEFACE MICROSOFT AND EMAIL SIGNATURE:

Arial Black

**ABCDEFGHIJKLMNOPQRSTUVQXYZ
abcdefghijklmnopqrstuvwxyz
1234567890{}:;,.'**

Arial Black Italic

ABCDEFGHIJKLMNOPQRSTUVQXYZ
abcdefghijklmnopqrstuvwxyz
1234567890{}:;,.'

TEXT TYPEFACE:

Times New Roman Regular

ABCDEFGHIJKLMNOPQRSTUVQXYZ
abcdefghijklmnopqrstuvwxyz
1234567890{}:;,.'

13

Notice how detailed the style guide is. It provides the horizontal and vertical options of the logo. It shows what the logo looks like in black and white and in color. It provides the specific RGB and Hex numbers for the colors in the color palette. It also provides the names of the fonts to be used.

After creating your logo and style guide, share it with anyone who will be using your logo—your website developer, your social media manager, the press, amongst others. This will ensure your logo and style are used consistently and as intended and will in turn help you build your brand recognition.

CONNECTING THE DOTS

Before finalizing your visual identity, get feedback on the designs from members of the target consumers you selected in Chapter 3. Share the designs with members of the broader stakeholder group you identified in Chapter 4 as well, especially to check for cultural sensitivities. (You don't want any elements of your logo or designs to unintentionally hurt or offend anyone.) Going forward, the visual identity you've developed in this chapter should be applied in all your marketing touchpoints—in the website you build in Chapter 6, the campaigns you build in Chapter 7, and the social media content you create in Chapter 8.

CHAPTER 6

Websites: How to Explain What You Do

We developed your brand's visual identity in Chapter 5, and the most important place it should be reflected is on your organization's website. It might be no surprise that a website is the most frequently referenced source where people seek information about a cause they might support—websites are used for this purpose more often than social media, family and even friends.

EXHIBIT 6.1 Sources Used Where People Search for Information About a Cause or Organization They Might Support

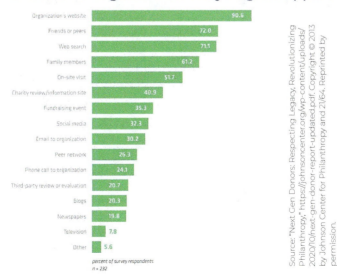

Source: "Next Gen Donors: Respecting Legacy, Revolutionizing Philanthropy," https://johnsoncenter.org/wp-content/uploads/2020/10/next-gen-donor-report-updated.pdf. Copyright © 2013 by Johnson Center for Philanthropy and 21/64. Reprinted by permission.

A website is a place where you can explain your organization's purpose (*why* you do what you do), your organization's mission (*how* you do what you do), and how people can support and get involved in your work. It is a place where you can organize what you want to communicate to your target consumers, potential partners, and volunteers, in much more depth than from what you could share in the limited space of a social media post.

Let's look at a few examples of how different organizations communicate their social impact work on their websites. Patagonia, a company that sells outdoor clothing and gear, devotes its website's homepage image to the causes it cares about:

Patagonia Homepage: https://www.patagonia.com/home/ July, 5th, 2020

Before you see Patagonia's weatherproof jackets, hiking boots, and backpacks, you see a stunning shot of a beautiful landscape. The day this screenshot was captured, the image was of the Arctic National Wildlife Refuge. While it's natural to think a for-profit corporation would want to spotlight the products it sells on the front page of its website, Patagonia instead leads with its purpose. Immediately someone visiting this website could think this is a company that cherishes the outdoors; selling outdoor clothing and gear just seems to be in service of that purpose. A nature-loving enthusiast could think, "This company's values align with mine. I trust them to make products in a sustainable way."

Ice cream brand Ben & Jerry's also devotes significant space on its homepage to its social impact efforts:

Ben & Jerry's Homepage: https://www.benjerry.com/ July, 5th, 2020

On the day this screenshot was captured, the brand was advocating for the Black Lives Matter movement, criminal justice reform, and the expansion of voting by mail options during the COVID-19 pandemic. We see ice cream on the homepage, but we also see a lot of passion from the brand for using its platform to educate its consumers on complex social issues. Consumers, investors, and even government legislators could see this website and feel, "I want to support this brand because I see that while it cares about profits, it also cares about people."

Now let's look at a nonprofit example. Take note at how Social Venture Partners India leads with a beautiful, engaging photo that draws the viewer in to whom its work serves:

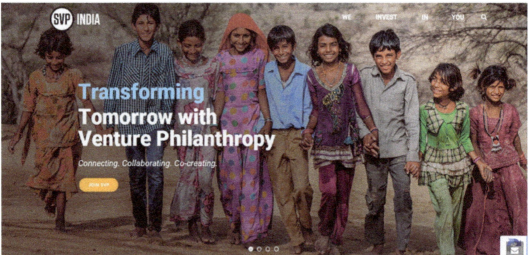

Social Venture Partners India Homepage: https://svpindia.org/ July, 5th, 2020

The tagline of "Transforming Tomorrow with Venture Philanthropy" married with the image of adorable, smiling children immediately lets the website visitor in on the organization's purpose and mission. A philanthropist could see this and think, "This is exactly what I want to invest in and be a part of as I build my legacy."

If you are a nonprofit leader, a professional-looking and well-organized website can help build confidence among a broad range of stakeholders that your organization is competent, experienced, and focused. If you are a marketer at a multinational corporation, showcasing your brand's purpose and social impact efforts prominently on your website can help build an emotional connection with your brand (versus a transactional one where only products are featured.) This can draw the reader in, inspiring a desire to learn more about what your organization does. Let's dive deeper into what makes for effective websites and then we'll cover steps on how to create one.

Characteristics of an Effective Website

▶ **The website has simple and intuitive navigation.** You don't want a person having to click multiple times within a website to find content he or she is looking for. The faster a user finds the information he or she needs, the faster that person can become a consumer, volunteer, or donor. Since you deepened your understanding of what is most important to your target consumers and customers from the exercises you did in Chapters 2, 3, and 4, prioritize this information on your website so it is easy to find.

▶ **The website loads quickly.** Sometimes high-resolution images and videos require more time to open or "load" on a website, which can lead to a user getting frustrated, getting distracted, and dropping off the site. Research or talk to your website developer on ways to overcome this, as technical tips and tricks evolve over time.

▶ **Some elements of the website are evergreen while some elements can be easily updated.** If you don't have time or money to hire someone who can manage and update your website regularly, it helps if the majority of your site contains content that does not change frequently. Your organization's purpose, mission, history, and contact information are likely elements you do not have to change often. You might have two or three areas of your website that require regular updating for things like upcoming events, new volunteer opportunities, and new staff and board members. Learn how to make edits to those sections and try not to mess with the evergreen portions of your website.

▶ **The website expresses the personality of the organization.** Did you notice how visually different the Patagonia, Ben & Jerry's, and Social Venture Partners India websites look from one another? Use the visual identity you created for your brand in Chapter 5 to help your website reflect your brand's unique personality and values.

Are you now excited to try creating your own website (or refresh an existing one)? Let's get started. The overall process can be broken down into the following four steps.

Step 1: Create a list of reference websites.

An easy place to start is to simply search online and note which websites you like. See which websites catch your eye, which ones seem easy to navigate, and which styles and formats might work for your organization. Use Exercise 6.1 to capture your thoughts.

EXERCISE 6.1   Create a List of Reference Websites

Reference Websites
These are three of my favorite websites and why I like them:
1.
2.
3.
These are the websites of organizations that do similar work to my social impact organization and what I like about them (this could include style, functionality, or navigation of the sites):
1.
2.
3.

This is what is missing from those sites (in terms of style, functionality, navigation) that I would like to see on my website:

1.

2.

3.

Step 2: Outline a website wireframe.

The next step in your web design process is to create a website wireframe. A wireframe is essentially a map of a website's pages. Think through how you might organize information you want to convey to your target consumers into easily digestible sections that can go on different pages of your website.

For nonprofits, common website pages include:

- ▶ Home
- ▶ Products (or Services or Programs)
- ▶ About Us
- ▶ Get Involved
- ▶ Donate

For corporations leading with social impact messaging, common website pages include:

- ▶ Home
- ▶ Products
- ▶ Sustainability (or Values)
- ▶ News (for press releases)

- ► Investors (for financial earnings reports)

- ► Where to Find Us

You can use these pages as a starting point—could they work for your organization? Review an example wireframe below in Exhibit 6.2. Then in Exercise 6.2 create a wireframe for your own social impact organization by adding and deleting boxes as needed (each box represents a page on your website).

EXHIBIT 6.2 Example Website Wireframe

EXERCISE 6.2 Create a Website Wireframe for Your Social Impact Organization

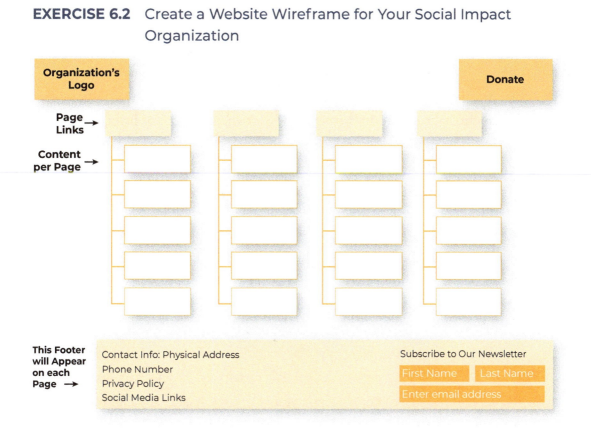

As you learned in Chapter 4, getting feedback on drafts of an idea can save you a lot of time in the future. Use this approach to solicit feedback on your drafted wireframe. Ask your target consumers and customers if the layout of the pages is how they would expect to navigate and find information about your products and services. While you can always add additional pages to the website later, thinking through the structure up front can help keep future content and page additions well organized.

Step 3: Create the website content.

The next step in your website development process is to decide what content goes on each page. You will likely want a balance of text, photos, and videos on your site so that it is visually interesting. Your job is to curate the content on the website, so it provides the right amount of detail to inform without overwhelming the website's visitor. If a reader wants to learn more, he or she can contact your organization. Here are some suggestions for content to include on key pages:

- ▶ **Home page:** As this is the first page site visitors will likely land on, you want to make a good first impression here. A captivating image (or two to three slider images) can draw someone in to learn more. Underneath that, you could give a high-level overview of the product or services you provide, the purpose and mission statements of your organization, facts about the cause you address, ways your organization measures success, and impact your organization has had. You could also include a section for logos of key recognizable partners and donors. This builds credibility for your organization as it signals that these people believe your work is impactful enough to invest in.

- ▶ **Product/Services page:** This page can provide a detailed description of the product or services your organization offers. If your organization offers products, you may want to include pricing information. If your organization provides services, you may want to include information about how one might be eligible for those services. Refer back to Chapter 1 and your social impact idea's 5 P's and decide how much of that information you think is appropriate to include on this page.

- **About Us page:** A page that lists names, photos, and short bios of key staff and board members can give website visitors a sense of how experienced and diverse the leadership team is. You can refer to Chapter 2 Exercise 2.2 to pull in this information. Be mindful though that if you work on sensitive issues like domestic violence, you might want to leave off specific names to protect the leadership team from angry or violent ex-spouses.

- **Get Involved page:** On this page you could include a list of upcoming events or volunteer opportunities. Sharing photos and recaps of past events can show people how fun it is to volunteer with your organization.

- **Donate page:** This page should have information on how the website's visitors can donate to your social impact organization. An integration with an online payments platform can make donating through the website quite easy. Including suggested levels of donations (for example $25, $50, $100) and what that donation enables (for example school supplies, internet for one month, or a metro card) can give a donor a sense of how his or her donation could be used. Adding an option to create a monthly recurring donation is a way to help the donor budget a manageable amount; this also helps a non-profit plan for consistent monthly revenue.

- **Footer:** The footer can consistently be included on each page of the website and can include things like your organization's contact information (address, phone number, and email address), links to your organization's social media sites, and a sign-up box for people to subscribe to your organization's email newsletter (if you have one).

See Exhibit 6.3 of how a nonprofit lays out the content it wants to present on each page of its website.

EXHIBIT 6.3 Website Content per Page for a Nonprofit That Provides Solar Powered Light to Homes in Villages via Sports Equipment

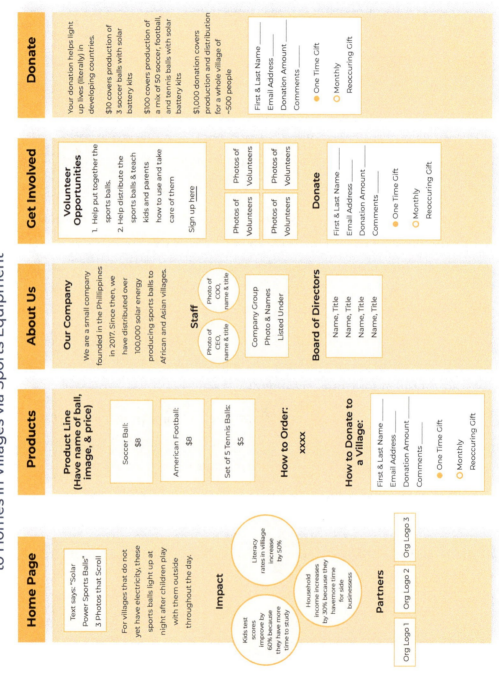

Home Page

Text says: "Solar Power Sports Balls" 3 Photos that Scroll

For villages that do not yet have electricity, these sports balls light up at night after children play with them outside throughout the day.

Impact

Kids test scores improve by 60% because they have more time to study

Literacy rates in village increase by 50%

Household income increases by 30% because they have more time for side businessess

Partners

Org Logo 1   Org Logo 2   Org Logo 3

Products

Product Line (Have name of ball, image, & price)

Soccer Ball: $8

American Football: $8

Set of 5 Tennis Balls: $5

How to Order: xxxx

How to Donate to a Village:

First & Last Name
Email Address
Donation Amount
Comments
● One Time Gift
○ Monthly
   Reoccuring Gift

About Us

Our Company

We are a small company founded in the Phillippines in 2017. Since then, we have distributed over 100,000 solar energy producing sports balls to African and Asian villages.

Staff

Photo of CEO, name & title

Photo of COO, name & title

Company Group Photo & Names Listed Under

Board of Directors

Name, Title
Name, Title
Name, Title
Name, Title

Get Involved

Volunteer Opportunities

1. Help put together the sports balls.
2. Help distribute the sports balls & teach kids and parents how to use and take care of them

Sign up here

Photos of Volunteers   Photos of Volunteers

Photos of Volunteers   Photos of Volunteers

Donate

First & Last Name
Email Address
Donation Amount
Comments
● One Time Gift
○ Monthly
   Reoccuring Gift

Donate

Your donation helps light up lives (literally) in developing countries.

$10 covers production of 3 soccer balls with solar battery kits

$100 covers production of a mix of 50 soccer, football, and tennis balls with solar battery kits

$1,000 donation covers production and distribution for a whole village of ~500 people

First & Last Name
Email Address
Donation Amount
Comments
● One Time Gift
○ Monthly
   Reoccuring Gift

Now write out the content and images you want to include for each of the pages of your website. (Recreate the chart in Exercise 6.3 if you need more space than what we have in this book.)

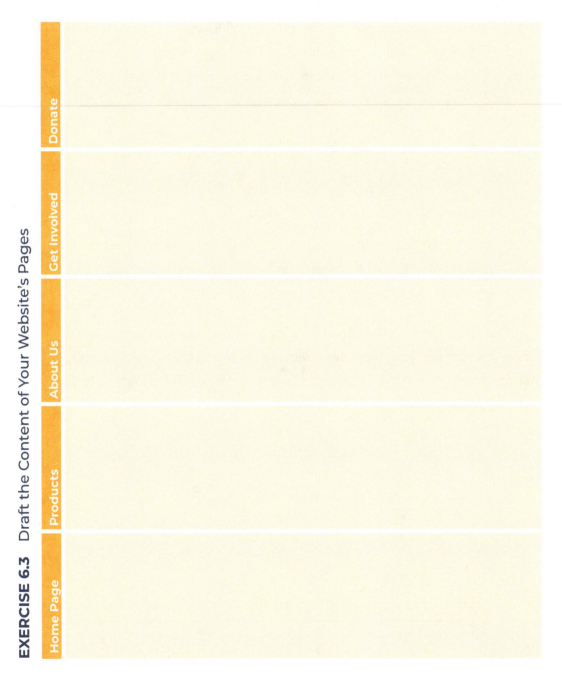

EXERCISE 6.3 Draft the Content of Your Website's Pages

Home Page	Products	About Us	Get Involved	Donate

Step 4: Build the website.

In this final step you complete the technical requirements to build the website and bring it online. If you have the technical know-how (or the patience to learn) of how to build a website yourself, you can use website building platforms such as WordPress, Wix, or Squarespace. On the other hand, you could hire a web developer to build the website for you. With either option, you will use the work you completed in Exercises 6.2 and 6.3 to populate the website's content.

There are two additional things you need to do to bring your website online:

- ▶ Purchase a hosting package. (This is a fee for holding the content of your site and making it available on the internet.)

- ▶ Select a domain name and pay an annual registration fee to use it. (A domain name is what people type into a browser to access your site, like www.xxxx.org.)

If you plan to hire a website developer, he or she might suggest a few sites from where you can purchase these two elements. When you are ready to onboard your website developer, use a brief (like the brief you created in Chapter 6) to share your website's requirements.

Organization Name
Website Brief

Briefing Date: April 17th
Client Name:
Website Developer Name:

Objective: Create a website with these 3 primary objectives:
1. Educate our target consumer (single mothers) whether they are eligible for our services
2. Show partners how they can engage with us
3. Attract donors and integrate with an online payments platform so it is easy to donate money directly through our website

Context: Our city's annual "Giving Day" (the day when our citizens are encouraged to donate to a nonprofit of their choice) is coming up on June 30th, so we are hoping to have our website online by then.

Websites We Like and Why:
- www.organizationA.org
- www.organizationB.org
- www.organizationC.org

The images on these sites are uplifting and not sad. They show mothers with 1 child and some with 2 or 3 children, which is reflective of the mothers we serve. We like that these websites use white space so that the content doesn't feel cluttered. We like the style of the dropdowns they use in the header links. And we like the mix of real photos (even though some are stock photography images) with graphic icons (like an icon of a graduation cap that symbolizes the organization's scholarship and continuing education program).

Website Wireframe: will be provided in another file

Content per Page: will be provided in another file

Considerations:
- Use the Style Guide provided for the website's visual identity.
- Our website domain name has been purchased through xx company.
- Our website is hosted on xx site.
- The Donations page should integrate with x payment services platform.

Timeline:

May 1 Round 1 Design draft delivered by developer

May 8 Round 1 Design feedback provided by client

May 22 Round 2 Design draft delivered by developer

May 29 Round 2 Design feedback provided by client

June 5 Round 3 Final layout of pages delivered by developer. If approved, developer starts coding the pages into a dummy site

June 12 All Team Members are invited to test the site in a dummy environment and send the developer notes on items needing updating via a Changes Tracker spreadsheet

June 24 Website Goes Live

Notice that brief includes mention of the style guide we learned how to create in Chapter 5. The style guide, the website wireframe, and the website's content per page should be sent to the website developer as addendums to the website brief. Try creating a website brief for your organization.

EXERCISE 6.4 Write a Website Brief

Organization Name
Website Brief

Briefing Date:
Client Name:
Website Developer Name:

Objective:

Context:

Websites We Like and Why:
-
-
-

Website Wireframe: will be provided in another file

Content per Page: will be provided in another file

Considerations:
-
-
-

Timeline:

Date Round 1 draft delivered by developer

Date Round 1 feedback provided by client

Date Round 2 draft delivered by developer

Date Round 2 feedback provided by client

Date Round 3 All Team Members are invited to test the site in a dummy environment and sends the developer notes on items needing updating via a Changes Tracker spreadsheet

Date Website Goes Live

The coding process with the developer should take roughly four to six weeks if you've done all the exercises leading up to this point. This accounts for time to spend on testing the website in a dummy environment (also known as a "sandbox" environment) to make sure the style, navigation, links, and donate functionality work to your liking before the website goes live. Remember to ask your website developer about search engine optimization (SEO) as well, which simply requires coding in some key words about your organization. This makes your website easier to find when people search the internet for services your organization provides. Review the tips in Chapter 5 for working with designers as those tips apply to working with website developers as well.

Once your website is up and running, you can use analytic tools, like Google Analytics, to see how people behave while on your site. Analytic tools can track the average time users spend on each page of the site, the aggregate gender and age range of the people visiting, where visitors are clicking and spending the most time, what percentage of visitors are making donations, and more. These tools aggregate data of your website visitors to protect personally identifiable information like names and addresses. It is important to review and analyze how people interact with your site so you can determine how effective it is in driving action (like generating donations or getting volunteers to sign up for events). More about marketing effectiveness and measurement will be covered in Chapter 10.

To the corporate marketers and students reading this book, helping a nonprofit with updating its website is an impactful way to use your professional skills to give back to your community. To the nonprofit leaders reading this book, leverage the talents of your board members and volunteers with this endeavor. Building a website is not difficult given the tools that exist today, but the process does require thoughtfulness. If you've done the exercises in the prior chapters, you have the content you need to clearly communicate to your stakeholders exactly what you do.

CONNECTING THE DOTS

Check if the content on your website is comprehensive by confirming you've included information about your 5 P's from Chapter 1. Check if your website is easy to navigate by watching a few members of the target consumer groups you chose in Chapter 3 click through the pages. Looking ahead, people will now have a website to visit to learn more about your organization after engaging with the marketing campaign you create in Chapter 7.

CHAPTER 7

Campaigns: How to Inspire and Engage

The job of a marketing campaign is to inspire and engage the human spirit to take a certain action. Sounds like a fun job, yes? This is the reason marketers become marketers. All of the strategic and foundational work you've been doing in the prior chapters have been in preparation for this main event.

A marketing campaign is a set of activities taken within a set time period with the intention of achieving a set goal. Marketing campaigns can be created for product launches, political candidates, announcement of new initiatives, fundraising for new libraries/hospital wings/arts centers, any number of things. With social impact marketing campaigns, of course, the set goal is to create some sort of positive impact for people or for the planet.

Luckily, you've likely been running campaigns your whole life. If you were a Girl Scout, you likely ran a campaign to sell your Girl Scout cookies to raise funds for your troop. The campaign probably lasted two months and you used all sorts of tactics to sell those cookies—you likely went door to door in your neighborhood to take cookie orders, you likely set up a little cookie stand at your local grocery store with other girls in your troupe, and you likely asked your parents to take cookie orders from their co-workers. When you became older, you created a campaign for yourself to land a job—you wrote a stellar resume, you got recommendation letters, you networked with people at the companies where you were interested in working, and you wore a nice suit to your interview. You might not have known it, but these were marketing campaigns.

In this chapter, we'll cover ways you can be intentional in the activities you choose to drive your social impact objectives. Notice we are talking about activities with an "s" as campaigns are more than just one viral video, one great speech, or one great event. To create real change, consumers must be informed, inspired and engaged with a cause before they consider taking meaningful action. This requires that campaigns reach consumers through multiple touchpoints. Moreover, as long as campaigns are set for a finite amount of time, they can run for a few days, a few weeks, or a few months. Companies with robust marketing departments run multiple campaigns throughout the year to keep their consumers engaged—Valentine's Day, spring, Earth Week, Mother's Day, summer, back to school, fall, the winter holidays, and New Years are all occasions to run a campaign. Some companies even create new campaign occasions like Discovery Channel's Shark Week and Starbucks' Pumpkin Spice Latte season. If campaigns become popular and achieve their goals, companies can choose to run them year after year, albeit for a set period of time.

How many campaigns your organization should run each year depends on the resources you have to create and execute them well. Large organizations employ creative agencies to think through a campaign's strategy and execution, but smaller organizations have to run them with the help of their staff and volunteers. Unlike the work you did in Chapter 6 to build a website you likely won't have to touch for a few years (minus a few updates for things like upcoming events), campaigns should be conducted much more frequently. While the goal of your website is to *inform*, the goals of your campaigns are to *inspire* and *engage*.

Given that there might be questions on the difference between social impact marketing campaigns and cause marketing campaigns, let's take a moment to discuss how we will define them in this book. For us, social impact marketing will have higher ambitions than traditional cause marketing. Cause marketing campaigns usually follow the format of "if you buy this product, we will donate a portion of the sales to a certain cause." While this is altruistic and commendable, it basically amounts to a reshuffling of monetary resources from the company to an underserved population.

With social impact marketing the goal is to have a positive impact on the world because your product exists, and the impact is not contingent on a sale. For example, if a water brand says, "For every water bottle purchased this month, we will donate $1 to building wells in rural villages," that is what we would consider a cause marketing campaign. If a water brand says, "This month, in celebration of World Water Day, we will release a series of short two minute videos to show how our water is sourced from local watersheds and is empowering women in those communities with sustainable livelihoods," that is what we would consider a social impact marketing campaign. A social impact marketing campaign prompts the mind's imagination of how a product itself has the power to bring about a positive change in society.

A beautiful example of a social impact marketing campaign is Ariel India's #ShareTheLoad campaign. As the leading laundry detergent brand in India, the brand decided to bring to light how women were progressing in their professional careers outside the home, yet they were still owning more than their fair share of household duties in the home. In a 2015 video advertisement, Ariel introduced a thought-provoking question, "Is laundry only a woman's job?" Instead of advertising the laundry detergent's functional attributes (like how well it cleans, its power to keep colors bright, or how affordable it is), the brand used its product to start a conversation on gender norms.

Ariel #Sharethe Load. Watch the video here: http://bit.ly/ArielSharetheLoad

In 2016, the brand extended the campaign. In a follow up video, we see a father observing his daughter come home from work, proceed to cook dinner, take a call from her office, change her son's shirt and put it in the laundry, tidy up his toys—all while her husband drank tea and watched television. The narration of the video is in the form of a letter the father writes to his daughter, in which he apologizes for the example he set when she was growing up. He acknowledges that she learned from what she saw, but that it wasn't too late for him to start helping her mother around the house. If not in the kitchen, he says he can at least help with the laundry, and in the end scene we see him loading the washing machine with his wife.

Ariel #DadsSharetheLoad. Watch the video here: http://bit.ly/DadsSharetheLoad

The end frame of the commercial added a twist to the original question by focusing on parents' role in setting an example for their children, "Is laundry only a mother's job? Dads #ShareTheLoad."

The campaign went viral and launched a national dialogue on the topic. Ariel embarked on a number of marketing activations to drive home the message of the campaign. It launched a His and Her Pack that essentially had the same washing instructions for both men and women. The brand partnered with clothing manufacturers to add a note to garments' wash care label that said, "Can be Washed by both

Men and Women #ShareTheLoad." It even partnered with matrimonial websites where, "Will you Share the Load in household chores with your partner Yes/No" was added to profiles. Over a million Indian men pledged to do so.

The campaign must have been hitting all three social impact marketing goals (building brand equity, increasing sales, and creating social impact) because the brand continued it in 2019. Ariel advanced the dialogue with a new question, "Are we teaching our sons what we've been teaching our daughters?"

Ariel #SonsSharetheLoad. Watch the video here: http://bit.ly/SonsSharetheLoad

In the video for this iteration of the campaign, a mother sits with her son in his messy room and takes a call from her daughter. Her daughter tells her she is thinking about leaving her job, and her mother asks her why. The English translation of their conversation goes something like this: "You are doing so well and we are so proud of you. Yes, your household responsibilities increased when you got married, but your husband can help you with those right? . . . What do you mean he doesn't know how? . . . Hmm, he might not know. The mistake is ours. We teach our daughters to stand on their own feet, but we don't teach our sons how to lend a hand." The mother asks her daughter to think about the situation again, says lovingly that she'll call her back in the evening, and they hang up. The son asks, "What happened mom?" The mom looks at her son and his messy room, picks up a laundry basket and says, "I made a mistake and I'm rectifying it." The video ends with a scene of the mom teaching her son how to do laundry and text that says, "Sons #ShareTheLoad."

The beauty of this campaign is how Ariel found a way for its product to help consumers take their own small steps toward advancing gender equality, an issue that sometimes seems too large to take on. Through masterful storytelling, social media efforts, partnerships and a multitude of other activations, Ariel built a campaign that touched the hearts of consumers and inspired marketers worldwide.

Characteristics of an Inspiring and Engaging Social Impact Marketing Campaign

- ▶ **The campaign is timely and relevant.** Campaigns that address current events and add a point of view to the cultural conversation of the times are inherently engaging because they prompt a dialogue. In 2018, Nike did this spectacularly with the launch of its Dream Crazy campaign. In the campaign's signature video, the narrator shares "calling a dream crazy is not an insult, it's a compliment." The video highlights footage of some "everyday athletes" with some of the greatest athletes of our times, like LeBron James and Serena Williams. Around the halfway mark in the video, it's revealed that the narrator is Colin Kaepernick, the football player whose kneeling during the singing of the national anthem sparked a massive dialogue around sports, politics, and race relations in the U.S. Kaepernick's kneeling was a form of peaceful protest, intended to bring awareness to the rampant police brutality directed towards Black Americans. His protests began in 2016 and started a movement within sports, though no team in the National Football League signed him in 2017. The narration of the video continues with Kaepernick saying, "Believe in something. Even if it means sacrificing everything." (*Watch the video here:* http://bit.ly/SocialImpactMktgDreamCrazy)

In the initial days of the video's launch, Nike's stock fluctuated. Some predicted Nike's decline, there were threats of a Nike boycott, and there were videos of people burning their Nike shoes. But Nike did not retract the video. The video made its television debut during the NFL season's opening day. The Dream Crazy campaign appeared on billboards, storefronts, and social media. Ten days after the launch of the campaign, Nike's stock price rose to the highest it had ever been. In February 2019, the campaign continued with a new video, Dream Crazier (*watch here:* http://bit.ly/SocialImpactMktg DreamCrazier), which celebrated trailblazing women in sports, this time narrated by Serena Williams. "The 'Dream Crazier' spot is the start of a journey celebrating women in sport ahead of soccer's biggest moment in France this summer," a Nike representative told AdWeek (The Washington Post, 2019). The big moment being referenced was the 2019 FIFA Women's World Cup. In May 2019, Nike was ready with Dream with Us (*watch here:* http://bit. ly/NikeDreamWithUs), a video featuring the U.S. Women's National Team. Each iteration of the campaign was timely and relevant.

▶ **The campaign is rooted in the brand's purpose.** In addition to a marketing campaign being timely and relevant, it must also be rooted in a brand's purpose. If not, the campaign risks being seen as an empty ploy to capitalize on a cultural moment. Take for example a situation where a brand might want to create a campaign for International Women's Day by making a significant donation to an organization that supports female entrepreneurs and women-owned businesses. If the brand hasn't taken any steps within its own organization to include women on its leadership team, a campaign like this would feel inauthentic. If a brand wants to join the conversation on the Black Lives Matter movement, a statement that reads "We believe Black Lives Matter" feels empty without addressing the advancement of Black people within its own company. These are examples from corporate brands, but the concept also applies to nonprofits. If a nonprofit's mission is to improve literacy rates, a month-long read-a-thon fundraising campaign more authentically advances its purpose over a 5k fundraising walk.

An example that marketers consistently consider as the gold standard in purpose-driven marketing is Dove's Campaign for Real Beauty. In 2006, Dove, a skin and hair care brand, developed a striking video titled Evolution. The video (*watch here:* http://bit.ly/SocialImpactMktgDoveEvolution) shows frame by frame the impact of a fresh-faced female model undergoing extensive hair and makeup. We see her photo taken. But the transformation doesn't end there. We then see her photo get photoshopped. We see the model's eyebrows lifted, her lips enlarged, and her neck elongated. We then see that photoshopped photo appear on a billboard advertising a makeup foundation. Text on the screen appears: "No wonder our perception of beauty is distorted." This video launched Dove's social impact work on building self-esteem in women and girls. Its campaigns started celebrating wrinkles and freckles and women of all shapes and sizes. The brand has invested in developing workshops and resources for parents, educators, and mentors on how to have conversations about body positivity. The brand's activations center around celebrating "real beauty." With such a steadfast grounding in its purpose, Dove launched a moving video during the COVID-19 pandemic that acknowledged the gravity of the moment while also advancing the mission of its campaign. Titled Courage is Beautiful, each shot of the video shows close-in profiles of healthcare workers' faces marked with visible imprints caused by long hours of wearing N-95 masks. The video ends with a note, "As a thank you, Dove is donating to Direct Relief to care for front-line healthcare workers in the U.S."

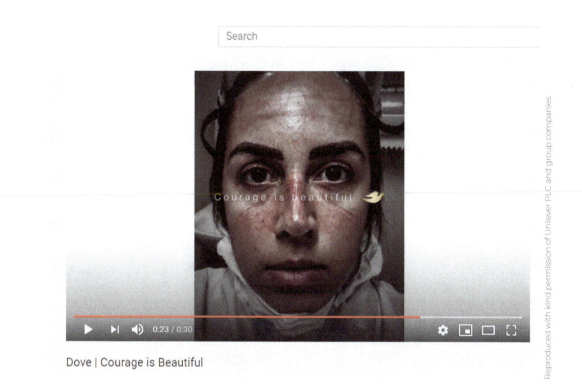

Dove | Courage is Beautiful

Dove Courage Is Beautiful. Watch the video here:
http://bit.ly/CourageIsBeautiful

Dove Real Beauty Sketches

If someone asked you to describe yourself, what would you say? Our body image takes such a battering that feeling beautiful can be hard – sometimes we just can't see beauty in ourselves at all. We think our self-esteem is in serious need of a boost.

The problem is, we're so bombarded by unattainable standards of beauty – in magazines, TV ads, on social media – that we undervalue the true beauty of ourselves. More than half of women globally agree that when it comes to how they look, they're their own worst critic. Our perception of ourselves is far less positive than it should be. And since we know that feeling beautiful is the first step to living happier, more confident lives, we decided to do something about it.

That something was a daring new beauty experiment: Real Beauty Sketches. We asked women to describe themselves to FBI trained forensic artist Gil Zamora from behind a mysterious curtain, who drew a portrait of them based on their description.

A random stranger was then asked to describe the same woman to Gil, to see how their description would differ. The result? Two completely different portraits. The one based on the stranger's portrayal was more beautiful, happier and more accurate. It proved exactly what we suspected: that you're more beautiful than you think. So to help inspire the millions of women around the world who don't see their own beauty, we created a film showing the women's reactions to their portraits, and the impact of their refreshed view of themselves.

"When I was asked to be a part of this film for Dove, I never imagined how different the two sketch portrayals would be," said Gil. "What has stayed with me are the emotional reactions the women had when they viewed the composite sketches hung side by side. I think many of these brave women realized that they had a distorted self-perception that had affected parts of their lives in significant ways."

> ❝ *What has stayed with me are the emotional reactions the women had when they viewed the composite sketches hung side by side. I think many of these brave women realized that they had a distorted self-perception that had affected parts of their lives in significant ways.*
>
> **Gil Zamora, FBI forensic artist**

|▷ An interview with Florence on her sketch

More than 50 million people viewed the Dove video within 12 days of its release. To date, Real Beauty Sketches has been viewed almost 180 million times. We want the film to continue to inspire every single one of the 80% of women who feel anxious about how they look to reconsider their view of their own beauty and remember: you're more beautiful than you think. It could be as easy as seeing ourselves through a stranger's eyes.

Explore more

Patches
Discover a beauty experiment

Inner Critic
Find out why women can be their own worst

Legacy
Legacy discovers if feeling beautiful is something we

Dove Real Beauty Sketches. Watch the video here:
http://bit.ly/SocialImpactMktgRealBeautySketches

The Ariel, Nike, and Dove campaigns mentioned are best in class. With these as inspiration, let's get started on creating campaigns for your social impact ideas.

Step 1: Create big ideas for campaign concepts.

Coming up with big ideas for marketing campaigns can feel intimidating, but there are exercises you can do to jumpstart your creativity. We will cover three of them:

1. Completing the Get To By framework

2. Completing the Think Say Do framework

3. Capturing trends important to your consumers

The **Get To By framework** helps you organize your thoughts around what actions you want your target consumers to take as a result of their engaging in your campaign. It goes like this:

Get (your target consumers)

To (do this action)

By (creating an engagement mechanism or tactics).

The following is a Get To By example for a campaign designed to encourage college students to engage with mental health resources on campus.

Get	To	By
Freshmen	Visit the mental health offices in the student health center	Offering free salad and sandwich lunches during mid-terms and finals weeks
Professors	Remind students of stress-relief tips	Emailing professors one slide they can share during their class presentations with stress-relief tips and info on where the college's mental health center is
College Administrators	Hire contract mental health therapists to meet the needs of international students who feel most comfortable speaking in another language	Hosting focus group sessions between international students and administrators so the latter can hear firsthand the challenges and apprehensions the former face when deciding if to approach the current mental health center

Think about what actions you want your target consumers to take as a result of engaging with your campaign and organize your thoughts in Exercise 7.1.

EXERCISE 7.1   Populate the Get To By Framework for a Campaign You'd Like to Create

Get	To	By
Target Consumer 1		

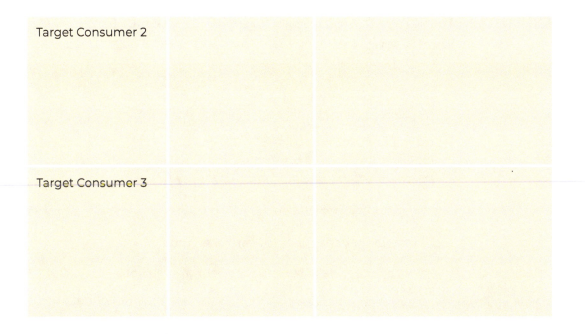

Target Consumer 2

Target Consumer 3

The **Think Say Do framework** is a similar framework, but it has some slight nuances. This framework focuses on the mental associations you'd like consumers to develop by engaging with your campaign. It also asks you to consider what you'd like consumers to say about your cause as a result of your campaign. The Think Say Do framework can help you map out what you want the target consumer to:

Think (in relation to your cause)

Say (about your product or cause)

Do (the action you want them to take around your cause)

The following is a Think Say Do example for a campaign designed to encourage more young adults to vote in upcoming elections.

EXHIBIT 7.2 Think Say Do Framework for a "We Create Our Future. We Vote!" Campaign

Think	Say/Share	Do
Voting is my civic duty	On social media the young adults add an image filter to their photo that says, "I did my job as a citizen today by voting—did you?"	The young adults vote
Voting is easy	Young adults share links on social media to where their closest voting station is	Young adults visit the website, register to vote if they haven't already, and then vote
I believe voting can make a difference	Young adults share a list on social media of the bills passed in the last few years that positively impacted the causes they care about	The young adults vote

Try filling out the framework for your social impact idea.

EXERCISE 7.2 Populate the Think Say Do Framework for a Campaign You'd Like to Create

Think	Say/Share	Do

With these two exercises, you should be clear on the actions you want your target consumers to take, so let's shift our focus to how we capture their interest. One way to do this is by first taking an audit of what they are already interested in. Talk to a few of your consumers and fill out the chart in Exercise 7.3.

EXERCISE 7.3 Capture Consumer Interests

What My Target Consumers Currently Care About
1. Television shows they currently watch:
2. Dance, music genres, or sports teams they are into:
3. Current events they are most interested in or are concerned about:
4. Celebrities they admire:
5. Trends in fashion or food they follow:

Now the brainstorming for campaign ideas can begin as you think through what actions you want your consumers to take and what is currently capturing their attention. This brainstorming can happen in a number of ways:

- Unstructured way: You can brainstorm campaign ideas with your team in a room together, or teammates can break off, individually come up with ideas, and then re-group to discuss together.

- Structured way: You could have your team sit at a table, set a timer for 60 seconds, and have each teammate think of as many ideas as they can. When the timer goes off, each person hands their paper to the person on their left. For the next 60 seconds each person builds on the ideas on the paper in front of them. Then you rotate papers to the left again. You can do this for three to five rounds.

Here's an example of what a brainstorm session could result in: You are trying to create a fundraising campaign for a local food pantry. Someone on your team mentions the "Great British Bake Off" show is trending on Netflix and is popular with your target consumer. The team decides a bake-off challenge with proceeds going to the food pantry would be a fun and engaging event. With this core big idea, the team then completes the following Steps 2–4 to flesh out the idea into a full campaign.

Therefore, try developing ten to twenty campaign ideas. Then narrow that list down to the top three to five that your team is drawn to. Build each of these ideas with a few more details to ensure they are (1) timely and relevant and (2) rooted in your organization's purpose. Jot down these ideas in Exercise 7.4.

EXERCISE 7.4   Develop a List of Campaign Big Ideas

Campaign Big Ideas
1.
2.
3.
4.
5.

Step 2: Test and pilot the campaign big ideas.

Recall from Chapter 4 the importance of testing an idea before bringing it to market. This applies to testing campaign ideas as well. Remember that not only will you want to seek feedback on your campaign ideas from your target consumers, you will want to get the opinion and buy-in of your campaign ideas from your broader stakeholders as well. These stakeholders can help ensure your campaign is culturally sensitive, and they can even champion or become participants in your campaign.

In sharing your campaign ideas, you might end up seeing ways to combine a few of the ideas. Or you might find one idea has everyone excited and rises to the top. Or you might find that your consumers and stakeholders aren't attracted to any of the ideas, after which you'll have to go back to Step 1 and do some more brainstorming.

How many resources you plan to put behind executing a campaign might dictate the rigor you put behind testing it. If the campaign doesn't require a high budget, a lot of time to execute, and is just planned to be launched in one geographic area, you might test the idea with a handful of consumers and stakeholders. If the campaign has a high budget and plans for a national or international rollout, you likely want to do more extensive testing on your big idea concepts. Your testing approach could include seeking both quantitative and qualitative data from a significant sample size of interviewees so that you have confidence in the campaign idea's potential to drive the change you wish to see. It is also a good idea that in addition to testing a campaign concept, you actually *pilot* the campaign in a relatively small environment. You could pilot your campaign idea in one city, with one retail channel, or on one social media platform, and see how it resonates with people before you put significant resources behind it.

Apply the research approach from Chapter 4 to testing your three to five big ideas. Capture your results in Exercise 7.5.

EXERCISE 7.5 Summarize Your Key Findings and Corresponding Recommendations for Each of the Big Ideas You Test

Research Findings and Recommendations for Big Idea 1	
Target Consumer Group 1	
Key Finding 1:	Recommendation 1:
Key Finding 2:	Recommendation 2:
Key Finding 3:	Recommendation 3:
Target Consumer Group 2	
Key Finding 1:	Recommendation 1:
Key Finding 2:	Recommendation 2:
Key Finding 3:	Recommendation 3:

Target Consumer Group 3

Key Finding 1:	Recommendation 1:
Key Finding 2:	Recommendation 2:
Key Finding 3:	Recommendation 3:

Research Findings and Recommendations for Big Idea 2

Target Consumer Group 1

Key Finding 1:	Recommendation 1:
Key Finding 2:	Recommendation 2:
Key Finding 3:	Recommendation 3:

Target Consumer Group 2

Key Finding 1:	Recommendation 1:
Key Finding 2:	Recommendation 2:
Key Finding 3:	Recommendation 3:

Target Consumer Group 3

Key Finding 1:	Recommendation 1:
Key Finding 2:	Recommendation 2:
Key Finding 3:	Recommendation 3:

Research Findings and Recommendations for Big Idea 3	
Target Consumer Group 1	
Key Finding 1:	Recommendation 1:
Key Finding 2:	Recommendation 2:
Key Finding 3:	Recommendation 3:
Target Consumer Group 2	
Key Finding 1:	Recommendation 1:
Key Finding 2:	Recommendation 2:
Key Finding 3:	Recommendation 3:
Target Consumer Group 3	
Key Finding 1:	Recommendation 1:
Key Finding 2:	Recommendation 2:
Key Finding 3:	Recommendation 3:

The results from testing these big idea options will probably give you an indication of which idea has the most potential for success. If there was more than one popular option, hold on to it—you might be able to use at another time. Select one big idea to move forward with as you now approach Steps 3 and 4.

Step 3: Set specific goals for the duration of the campaign.

Setting targets for your campaigns around the three social impact marketing goals (building brand equity, increasing sales, and creating positive impact) can help keep you focused on what you want to achieve before, during, and after the campaign. For purposes of this book, we will expand our goal of "build brand equity" to "build brand equity and awareness." Companies with large marketing insights budgets have tools to measure brand equity scores pre- and post-campaign. But given those studies can be costly, we will measure how much awareness we are able to create with a campaign as a proxy to how much a campaign increases brand equity. Also, given that some social impact ideas do not have a product sales component, we will broaden the goal of "increase sales" to "increase sales or engagement." Finally, we will expand "positive impact" to include "positive impact or positive behavior change." These definitions will be discussed more in Chapter 10.

Setting goals for a campaign can help motivate people towards achieving certain milestones. It can also help set benchmarks for future campaigns. If a campaign over-delivers on its goals, the team might set higher goals the following year. If none of the campaign goals are achieved, the team might set more realistic goals for the following year.

Metrics used to determine if goals are being met are called ***key performance indicators***. See the example in Exhibit 7.3 for the KPIs set for a common-sense gun laws campaign.

EXHIBIT 7.3 Goals and KPIs for a Common-Sense Gun Laws Campaign

Social Impact Marketing Goal	Key Performance Indicators
Create Positive Impact or Positive Behavior Change: Enact common-sense gun laws in all states.	Number of bills/laws passed
Increase Sales or Engagement: Have 150 people contact each senator and representative in their state Have 15,000 people sign petitions in each state to share their support of the proposed common-sense gun laws	Number of people who contact their government representatives Number of people who sign the petitions
Build Brand Equity or Awareness: Get 50,000 Likes, Hearts or the Equivalent and 1,000,000 impressions on social media during the 6-month campaign.	Collective number of "likes" and impressions on three social media platforms

Determine what goals and KPIs you want to set for your campaign in Exercise 7.6.

EXERCISE 7.6 Choose Campaign Goals and Their Key Performance Indicators for Your Social Impact Campaign

Social Impact Marketing Goal	Key Performance Indicators
Create Positive Impact or Positive Behavior Change:	
Increase Sales or Engagement:	
Build Brand Equity or Awareness:	

Step 4: Plan for and launch the campaign in a 360 degree fashion.

As mentioned previously, a campaign is more than one event. It's more than one viral video, one sales event, or one interview. Consumers need to hear a message multiple times (a rule of thumb is approximately 5–7 times) before it is internalized. Engaging with consumers through multiple tactics and touchpoints is called a 360 degree activation. Therefore, planning multiple channels for the consumer to receive a message—be it through social media, TV, podcasts, billboards, etc.—is a sign of a well thought through campaign. 360 degree activation plans are usually represented in a circular wheel like in the image below.

EXHIBIT 7.4 360 Degree Marketing Campaign Activation Wheel

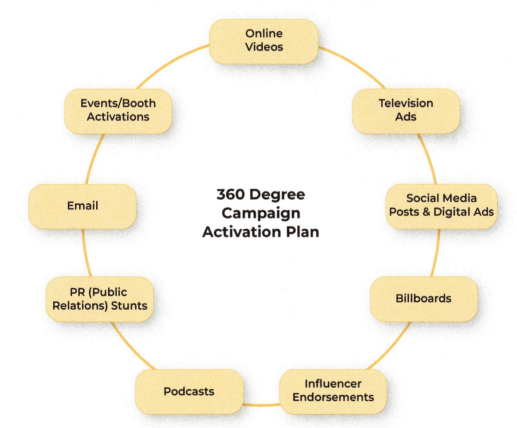

Below is an image of the 360 degree campaign activation plan for the Lay's Artesana's compostable packaging mentioned in Chapter 4. Take note of how the brand created a key visual and tagline "Un Pequeño Paso Para Un Mundo Mejor" (*"A small step for a better world"*) at the center of its campaign, and then replicated that visual and message through various digital, PR, on-pack, and in-store activations. The brand also took the advice of recycling partner, Triciclos, throughout the planning process. TriCiclos moreover helped to coordinate collection of the compostable bags so that they could be disposed of in a proper collection stream and not end up in a landfill.

Chile Sustainable Packaging Pilot 360 Campaign

If we pick up with the bake-off challenge big idea from before, a 360 degree activation plan for that could look like: chefs hosting bake-off challenges at their restaurants throughout the city for a month, winners being announced and interviewed on local TV stations, volunteer days at the food pantry to physically stock the shelves, local grocery stores selling baking kits that have a tag mentioning the bake-off challenge details…the possibilities are endless.

As you think through all the different ways you can engage your consumers and stakeholders around your campaign's big idea, here are even more channels to consider:

▶ **Email:** You can send information about your campaign to people in your email distribution list. You also can ask partner organizations to share your campaign details in their email distribution lists as well.

▶ **Social media:** Leverage social media to get the word out about your campaign. (You will learn more about social media in Chapter 8.)

▶ **Public Relations:** If you have any connections with celebrities and influencers that care about the cause you work on, see if they could reach out to their followers with a message about your campaign. (You will learn more about PR in Chapter 9).

▶ **Billboards:** If it's appropriate and useful, see if you can get your campaign message on billboards, signs, and bus stops.

▶ **Podcasts:** Which podcasts address your social impact topic? Which podcasts are popular with your target consumer? Reach out to the host of those podcasts to see if they could have you on.

▶ **Videos:** Short videos can be shared easily online.

▶ **Events:** You can set up a booth at events or conferences to leverage their foot traffic to share information about your campaign.

With all these options at your disposal, get creative and think through a 360 degree activation plan for your big idea.

EXERCISE 7.7   Create a 360 Degree Campaign Activation Wheel

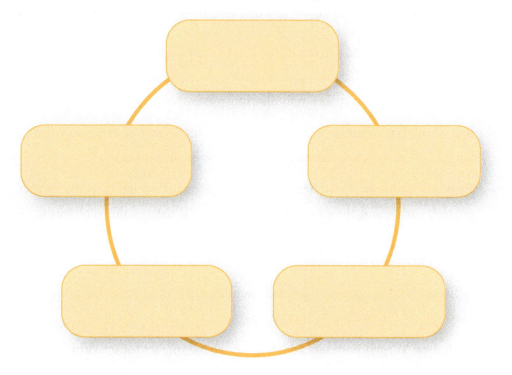

As a bonus, you might want to ride the momentum of national or international events that relate to your cause. For instance, if you have a campaign that is focused on women's empowerment, you might plan an activation around International Women's Day that falls on March 8 each year. If you are working on a campaign to clean up the environment, you might want to plan an event around Earth Day which falls on April 22 annually. The added press around these key events can boost the coverage and mindshare your campaign could capture. List any key events or holidays that connect with your cause in Exercise 7.8.

EXERCISE 7.8   List National or Global Events Related to Your Cause

Date	Event

You now know the fundamentals of how to engage people with your social impact product or idea. While not everyone can work at a nonprofit, most people want to do good. Make this easy for them. Inspire your consumers through your campaigns and help them become a part of the change you wish to see in the world.

CONNECTING THE DOTS

Now that you have ideas for marketing campaigns, think about the partners you identified in Chapter 1 and how you might include them in your 360 degree activation plans. Going forward in Chapters 8 and 9 you will learn how to use social media and PR, respectively, to amplify your campaigns.

CHAPTER 8

Social Media: How to Stay Top of Mind

Do you have $5.6 million to spend on a Super Bowl ad? If so, you could reach 100 million viewers. Or do you at least have $500,000 to air an ad during the FIFA World Cup Women's Final? There you could reach 26 million viewers. Those were the price tags of airing a 30-second advertisement during those sporting events in 2020 and 2019, respectively. If you do not have that kind of money, though, how does *free* sound to you?

This is the seductive part of social media—it's essentially a free way for your message to reach millions of people. And this price tag is very attractive for nonprofit and social impact organizations that try to spend most of their budget on programming and direct services over costly TV commercials.

Any brand can easily create a free account, quickly upload content, and connect with its consumers on a social media platform. Frequent and consistent communication via social media can help keep a brand top of mind with consumers. At the time of this publication, Facebook, YouTube, Instagram, Twitter, and TikTok are some of the most popular social media platforms in the world. With people spending over two hours a day on social networks and messaging apps globally (per the GlobalWebIndex's Social Flagship Report 2020) that's a good amount of time to capture mindshare from potential donors and volunteers. And if you can capture a user's attention in social media, you've increased your chances of getting them to hit a Donate Now or Learn More button. Doesn't this seem easier and quicker than planning a large fundraising gala?

But what happens when a social media post by a nonprofit's executive director only gets a disappointing three or four Likes or Hearts? What happened to the millions of potential followers and donors?

This situation is a common occurrence amongst growing nonprofits. Without the budget to hire a marketer, the task of posting social media content falls to a nonprofit's CEO, someone who likely hasn't had extensive training on social media marketing. Large brands can also suffer from low engagement on social media when they post content around their social impact efforts, especially if those posts feel disjointed from the brands' usual content. Given that there are many textbooks, courses, and even free online videos you could watch to learn best practices in social media marketing, this book will focus specifically on elements to keep in mind for social impact content.

Social media works best for social impact marketing when it's an integrated element of a brand's 360 degree campaign activation plans (which you learned how to create in Chapter 7). This approach is beautifully illustrated in a campaign by Doritos, a global snack brand. Since 2015, Doritos had been championing LGBTQ+ rights with a yearly campaign called Doritos Rainbow. In 2019, the Doritos Rainbow campaign in Mexico focused on celebrating the transgender community with a unifying campaign tagline "#DesbloqueemosElAmor" (literal English translation is "Let's Unblock Love").

As a brand positioned "for the bold," Doritos stated, "We believe that something as BOLD as LOVE should never be blocked, not by you, nor by me, nor by any individual." The brand created a full 360 degree campaign activation which included participating in Mexico City's Pride Parade, hosting workshops with nonprofit partner Cuenta Conmigo, and launching stunning limited-edition packages designed by Vicente Arias, a member of the Doritos design team. (Vicente's drag queen persona, Nina de la Fuente, appeared on the right-most packaging image that follows.)

To bring attention to the campaign and amplify its efforts, Doritos made an intentional effort to focus its social media content on three areas:

1. The concept of "unblocking love"

2. The images of the new limited-edition bags so consumers could look out for them in stores

3. The events it was hosting throughout the month

While the brand could have simply posted "Happy Pride Month" or "we believe in equality," on its social media accounts, this content was so much more engaging. With these focused efforts, Doritos was able to reach 35 million people on social media in Mexico, the highest reach of any of its previous digital campaigns.

These exciting results become a possibility when a brand takes time to invest in creating a thoughtful social media strategy. Let's look at some additional best practices for creating engaging social media content before we embark on creating a strategy for your own social impact organization.

Characteristics of Effective Social Media

▶ **Social media should help people be social.** Think about what contributed to the ALS Ice Bucket Challenge of 2014 becoming such a viral sensation on social media. People tagged multiple friends with the challenge to dump a bucket of ice on their heads, with an accompanying video for proof, to raise awareness and donations for ALS (amyotrophic lateral sclerosis—a progressive neurodegenerative disease). It was a fun stunt with just the right amount of effort required to make it meaningful and memorable. The social nature of friends loving to see their friends (and celebrities!) take the challenge made these videos shareable and engaging, and video views helped the content trend with social media algorithms.

- **Social media should provide users value.** Posts that entertain, make people laugh, make them think, or help them learn something new are posts your followers will want to share. The brands you follow on social media probably do one if not more of these things. Some people ask, "How do you create viral videos? I just need one viral video so that people will donate to my cause!" The answer is you don't "create viral videos." You create good content which people want to share, then it goes viral. Think—is your social media content valuable and worth sharing?

So, while social media can be "free," it requires significant time and effort to do well. With this understanding, let's embark on the steps to develop your social media strategy.

Step 1: Research the social media platforms your target users are on.

It'll be difficult (and inefficient) to post content and manage conversations on every new social media site, so focus your efforts on the platforms your target consumers and customers are engaging with most. In 2021, the baby boomer generation in the U.S. is mainly on Facebook; Gen X and Millennials are predominately on Facebook and Instagram; and Gen Z is mainly on Instagram, Tik Tok, and Snapchat. See Exhibit 8.1 for an example of how you can easily survey a few of your consumers to note what platforms they use most often.

EXHIBIT 8.1 Social Media Platforms Frequented by Target Stakeholders of a Girls' Sports and Life Skills Program

(Note: The program's consumers are the girls participating in the program, and the program's customers are the parents and donors who fund it.)

Social Media Platform Research	
Target Group 1 Customers: Parents	Most parents and caregivers in the neighborhood for this program are ages 40+. When surveyed they reported they mostly use Facebook.
Target Group 2 Consumers: Girls ages 7–18	Since the age limit to have a social media account is 13, only those girls 13+ will be communicated with through social media. The girls in this age range of this neighborhood told the program director that they are mostly on Instagram and TikTok.
Target Group 3 Customers: Donors (including board members and volunteers)	Donors told the program leadership that they mainly use Facebook and email to stay in touch with friends and learn updates from organizations.

© Monkey Business Images/Shutterstock.com

Populate the chart below after asking a few members of your target consumer groups which social media platform they use most often.

EXERCISE 8.1 Research Social Media Platforms Your Target Consumers Use Most Often

Social Media Platform Research	
Target Group 1 Consumer/Customer:	
Target Group 2 Consumer/Customer:	
Target Group 3 Consumer/Customer:	

Step 2: Determine your social media personality.

It's engaging when a brand's unique personality and tone of voice shines through on their social media accounts. Look at the chart in Exercise 8.2 below and circle four to five of the words that you'd like to reflect your brand's personality. These words should influence the tone of voice you use when writing your social media posts.

EXERCISE 8.2 Circle Four to Five Words That Reflect Your Brand's Personality (or Add Your Own Options)

My Brand's Social Media Personality			
Happy/Cheerful	Factual/Academic/Data-Driven	Casual/Conversational	Youthful
Serious/Somber	Faith Forward/Spiritual	Inviting/Inclusive	Visionary
Playful	Edgy/Trendy	Urgent	Hopeful
Funny	Personal	Compassionate	Collaborative
(Add your own options here)			

Step 3: Decide the types of content and themes you want to post about.

Social media algorithms prioritize content they show in news feeds from accounts that post with a frequent and consistent cadence. Therefore, a good rule of thumb is to post content at least two to three times per week. Given this level of frequency however, it could become difficult to generate creative content ideas the day of the week you've committed to posting. Therefore, a good plan is to think through the types of content and themes you want to post about ahead of time. Types of content you could consider include short video clips of volunteer events, inspirational quotes, or even thought-provoking questions that encourage responses on the social media platform. Read through the content ideas in Exercise 8.3 and circle the ones you think could help create interest and engagement around your social impact organization and cause.

EXERCISE 8.3 Circle the Content Themes You Want to Share in Your Social Media Posts

Content Themes for Social Media Posts			
Informational videos of how to use the products or services your organization provides	Short videos of testimonials from clients your organization serves	A challenge that requires people to tag a friend	Informative facts about the cause your organization works on
Information of what a donation covers (e.g., a $500 donation covers tuition for a continuing education course)	Invitation to join an upcoming volunteer event	Short videos of volunteers working on projects	A behind-the-scenes video of how your organization does what it does
Inspirational quotes	Simple tips on how people can get involved in your organization	Images of partner organizations coming to help during an event	Short video messages from the leadership team or board members
(Add your own options here)			

In the next exhibit we see how the content ideas can then be organized by what we think will resonate most with each target consumer group.

EXHIBIT 8.2   Social Media Content Themes Organized by Target Consumers of a Girls' Sports and Life Skills Program

Social Media Content Themes Organized by Target Consumer				
Target Group 1 Consumer: Parents/ Caregivers	Short videos of testimonials from clients your organization serves	Inspirational quotes	Facts about the cause your organization works on	Images or videos of how to use the products or services your organization provides
Target Group 2 Consumer: Program Recipients/Girls	What to bring to class today (ex. homework, sports gear)	Inspirational quotes	Message from girls who have graduated from the program	Study tips or sports tips on topics covered during the week
Target Group 3 Consumer: Donors and volunteers	Simple tips on how people can get involved in your organization	Images of partner organizations coming to help during an event	Short video messages from the leadership team or board members	Short videos of volunteers working on projects
	A challenge that requires people to tag a friend	Invitation to join an upcoming volunteer event	A behind-the-scenes video of how your organization does what it does	Information of what a donation covers (e.g., a $100 donation covers sports uniforms and gear for 1 year)

Recall the target consumer and customer groups you chose to focus on in Chapter 3. Map out the social media content you think will be more interesting and engaging for them in Exercise 8.4.

EXERCISE 8.4 Map Social Media Content Themes by Your Target Consumers

Types of Content for Social Media Posts Organized by Target Consumer				
Target Group 1 Consumer/ Customer:				
Target Group 2 Consumer/ Customer:				
Target Group 3 Consumer/ Customer:				

Step 4: Write out your social media posts a month in advance.

While you can post spontaneously if an occasion calls for it, it also helps to draft your posts in advance. Think through what days you want to post content for each target audience. See how the sample schedule in Exhibit 8.3 can give you a glimpse of how you are communicating with your target throughout a month.

EXHIBIT 8.3 Social Media Posting Schedule for a Girls' Sports and Life Skills Program

	Sunday	Monday	Tuesday	Wednesday	Thursday	Friday	Saturday
Week 1	Girls	Parents		Girls	Parents		
Week 2	Girls	Parents		Girls	Parents		
Week 3	Girls	Parents		Girls	Parents		
Week 4	Girls	Parents		Girls	Parents		Monthly email to donors & volunteers

Monthly Social Media Calendar Posting Schedule

Instagram icon © tanuha2001/Shutterstock.com; Facebook icon © rvlsoft/Shutterstock.com; email icon © mamanamsai/Shutterstock.com

Decide what days would be most appropriate to post on given your organization's work and target audiences, and create a posting schedule in Exercise 8.5.

EXERCISE 8.5   Social Media Monthly Posting Schedule

Monthly Social Media Posting Schedule							
	Sunday	Monday	Tuesday	Wednesday	Thursday	Friday	Saturday
Week 1							
Week 2							
Week 3							
Week 4							

You've taken this much effort to plan, now go the extra mile and actually write out your posts. Think about the text, images and videos, and any people you want to tag or hashtags you want to include for each post. If you are in the midst of running a marketing campaign (which you learned how to do in Chapter 7) be sure to include posts about the campaign as well. Have your legal and/or public relations teammates check the posts to ensure they are accurate, appropriate, and culturally sensitive.

EXHIBIT 8.4   Social Media Post Drafts for a Girls' Sports and Life Skills Program

	Day to Post	Post Text	Image or Video	People to Tag/Hashtags to Include
Week 1	(Monday) Parents :	This week the girls will be learning about budgeting. What are some of your favorite budgeting tips?	Photo of girl in our program when she was younger putting money into a piggy bank	#FinancialLiteracyMonth
	(Thursday) Parents:	Review your daughter's homework and talk about budgeting goals together.	Photo of one of our moms with her daughter looking over a budget	#FinancialLiteracyMonth
	(Sunday) Girls:	Think about 3 things you want to save up money for.	Photo of girl in our program making a list	#budgeting
	(Wednesday) Girls:	Bring your budgeting homework today.	Photo of girl in our program putting her homework in her bag	#budgeting
Week 2	(Monday) Parents :	Volunteers needed! We need two parents for this week's practices to pass out snacks and help the coaches.	Video of one of our program's parents handing out snacks	#WeLoveOurVolunteers
	(Thursday) Parents:	It's game day! Come cheer on the girls tonight at 6 pm!	3 second video of crowd cheering	#gameday
	(Sunday) Girls:	"This program taught me how I could afford college and land the job of my dreams."—quote from program graduate	Quote card with visual identity elements	#FinancialLiteracyMonth
	(Wednesday) Girls:	Remember to bring your knee pads to practice today.	Photo of girl in our program putting knee pads in her duffle bag	#volleyball
Week 3	(Monday) Parents :	If you have chores your girls can do to earn some dollars, they will be fundraising $50 each for the state tournament.	Photo of girl in our program vacuuming	#volleyball
	(Thursday) Parents:	Tournament sign ups are now open here: (Link to sign up)	Image of sign up form	#volleyball

	(Sunday) Girls:	With a partner, practice low, high, and quick passes this weekend.	5 second video demo	#volleyball
	(Wednesday) Girls:	"Genius is 1% talent and 99% hard work."—Albert Einstein	Quote card with visual identity elements	#motivation
Week 4	(Monday) Parents :	This week talk to your child about saving for college.	Short video clip of past progarm graduates at their colleges	#college
	(Thursday) Parents:	Watch this 5 min video on how to set a college savings fund. (Link to video)	Video screen shot	#college #budgeting
	(Sunday) Girls:	"Don't be afraid. Be focused. Be determined. Be hopeful. Be empowered."—Michelle Obama	Image of Michelle Obama or a short video clip of her remarks	#ReachHigher
	(Wednesday) Girls:	Read this article of our graduate Lauren who is now in college studying law. (Link to article)	Image of article	Tag Lauren #college
Last Saturday of the Month	Donor Newsletter Content	— Program Recap/High-lights: The girls learned about budgeting and saving this month. — Impact: We have 30 girls in the program this semester and they are all making A's and B's in school. — Funds Raised thus far: We have raised 80% of the funds needed to participate in the state volleyball tournament. — Ways to Get Involved: Sign up to help teach a bike safety course next month.		

Following the example above, write out a month's worth of content for your organization. This could require a few pages, so complete this exercise outside of this book.

Content Tips

- ▶ Tag people and places in your posts. The more people see their friends in a post, the more likely they are to engage with the post.

- ▶ Make the user want to click "Learn More." Your posts do not have to be long. Just post enough content to draw people in. If people want to learn more, they will navigate to your Learn More button or to your website.

- ▶ Use the Style Guide you developed in Chapter 5 to extend your brand's visual identity to your social media posts, which becomes another way to continue building brand equity.

- ▶ Post well-lit photos that clearly tell a story of what is happening in the image.

- ▶ Try not to show messy piles of donations that need sorting. While it may seem this strategy could attest to the dire need for volunteers, try to put your best foot forward as most people hope for a pleasant volunteer experience.

Clockwise from top left: © BAZA Production/Shutterstock.com, © Salena Stinchcombe/Shutterstock.com, © MCarper/Shutterstock.com, © Dragana Gordic/Shutterstock.com

Step 5: Post your social media content and use it to keep the conversation going.

In this final step, post your content. Many social media platforms will allow you to upload several posts at once and schedule when they get posted live. In this way, you can schedule a month's posts all at once and not have to remember to do so every few days. Once your content goes live, monitor the comments you receive. Respond to the comments and engage in conversation with your followers. If certain posts get significant engagement, you might consider spending money to boost those posts, essentially helping those posts appear in more newsfeeds on the platform. Moreover, with the advanced targeting capabilities of social media platforms, you can choose certain audiences you'd like your boosted posts or ads sent to. These audiences can be based on certain criteria like age, interests and geography. There are so many features of social media that tips and tricks are hard to capture, especially since it is a space that is constantly evolving.

As we have progressed through the last few chapters you might have noticed that a website is a platform you might have to refresh only every few years, campaigns likely span several months, but social media is something you have to monitor daily. If you want to give it a try, set your expectations based on the effort you plan to put in.

CONNECTING THE DOTS

Review the social media content you've drafted to see if it includes information about your 5 P's from Chapter 1 that would appeal to the target consumers you prioritized in Chapters 2 and 3. Include your social media account links on the website you created in Chapter 6 and make sure your content also includes information on how to get involved in any campaigns you might have built in Chapter 7.

CHAPTER 9

Public Relations: How to Manage Your Reputation

"Our nonprofit is this city's best kept secret," said one board member to a nonprofit's CEO. Please let the gravity of that statement sink in. This is not something to be proud of. John D. Rockefeller, American businessman and philanthropist, has been quoted as saying, "Next to doing the right thing, the most important thing is to let people know you are doing the right thing." This is the role of public relations.

Unlike in other chapters, there is no special twist on how social impact organizations need to approach public relations—they simply need to start prioritizing it.

Many people get confused with the difference between public relations and marketing. Many small organizations combine them into one person's job. Many large organizations also combine public relations and marketing departments under one chief marketing and communications person.

These two functions work closely together but they are not the same. While marketers develop the details of what a product or idea is and how to bring it to life, the public relations experts manage how to communicate that with the world, with the *public*. PR professionals develop **key messages** about a new product or campaign that can be tailored for different stakeholders, events, and channels. These key messages are talking points that can be communicated to the masses via press releases to the media or via outreach to influencers and celebrities. Proactively reaching out to others to write and talk about your idea, product, or organization can help your message reach so many more people than if you just let word of mouth take its course.

Traditionally PR has been seen as a function that can manage the image and reputation of a company. But PR can also play a huge role in social impact. Richard Edelman, CEO of Edelman, the largest PR firm in the world, delivered a speech on September 24, 2020 in which he described the evolving role of the PR industry:

> *Our communications must follow meaningful actions . . . image and persuasion matter less than tangible commitments and accountability. . . .*
>
> *Our success will be measured not only by business impact but also improvements in society. . . .*
>
> *Controlling the narrative is a futile endeavor. Broad community story development and validation is better . . . Our communications must be relatable and honest.*
>
> *Telling only good news is not sufficient. Not truthful. We need to offer a full picture based on facts and transparency. Side effects included.*
>
> *Moreover, it is our responsibility to help correct misinformation as a conduit of reliable information attributed to independent sources.*
>
> *. . . not every client is worthy of our attention and support; we are not lawyers, we are actually public advocates.*
>
> Excerpts from a speech delivered on September 24, 2020, by CEO Richard Edelman, posted on Edelman's website.

This role of public advocate can be seen in action with an example from PR agency Porter Novelli and its work with Street Grace, a nonprofit in Atlanta, Georgia, that works to *"mobilize communities to eradicate the Commercial Sexual Exploitation of Children."* The nonprofit knew that more than 3,600 children were being sold into sex slavery in the state of Georgia each year. So, in 2019 Porter Novelli partnered with Street Grace's marketing agency BBDO to create a strategy to bring awareness to this problem. They took advantage of the added attention Atlanta was going to receive for hosting the Super Bowl that year and used the city's traffic to talk about "trafficking."

The organizations lined Atlanta streets with 72 school buses, enough to hold 3,600 schoolchildren, to visually represent the staggering numbers of this problem. They used traffic signs, social media, and traditional media to drive conversation about the topic. Their media outreach efforts secured 120 broadcast and radio segments, 400 placements across all types of media, and achieved 210 million impressions. And what was the social impact? One month after the campaign, 33 people were arrested on sex trafficking charges in Atlanta.

Porter Novelli Street Grace. Watch a video recap of the campaign here:
https://www.porternovelli.com/project/street-grace/

While this is an example of how PR can help amplify and advance the positive impact work of a nonprofit, this next example illustrates how PR can help a social impact organization manage a situation when things go awry.

In 2012, the Lance Armstrong Foundation's namesake professional cyclist was exposed for doping by the U.S. Anti-Doping Agency. The organization had been well known for raising significant money for prostate cancer research. You might even remember the organization from the micro donations it raised through sales of its iconic yellow Livestrong wristbands. The doping scandal was about to become the largest PR crisis the organization had faced. The threat of losing donors was very real. (Case in point, after helping the foundation raise more than $100 million, Nike ended its partnership with the nonprofit in 2013.)

A few months later at the PRSA (Public Relations Society of America) Spring Conference in Austin, Texas, the foundation's PR team shared their lessons from confronting the crisis. They were able to manage the situation by "allowing donors, supporters and friends to speak on behalf of the organization" and by amplifying "stories of their everyday recipients of the foundation" (Walcher, 2013).

In November 2012, the organization also changed its name to Livestrong. "We're an organization that made a decision to stand on our own two feet, and it's not about one person and it's not about that person's celebrity," Livestrong Chairwoman Candice Aaron told USA Today in a May 2016 article. "It's about all the people we serve. . . . We feel like we don't need a celebrity, because the heroes of Livestrong are those people you encounter every day who are fighting cancer." Nine years later, at the time of this publication, the foundation is still providing resources to cancer survivors and their loved ones.

© Photo Works/Shutterstock.com

Hopefully, your organization won't have to face a situation like this, but we will discuss how to prepare for a crisis in Step 4.

The Street Grace and Livestrong cases illustrate what a critical function PR can play for a social impact organization. If you are a marketer at a large, global corporation, your PR team could help secure and coordinate speaking engagements to discuss your organization's social impact efforts at conferences like the World Economic Forum or a United Nations summit. The PR team could also help secure media coverage in national and international news outlets. If, on the other hand, you work at a small nonprofit and do not have the resources to hire a PR specialist, you might be able to enlist the help of your board of directors. Given your board members' connections within the community, they might have contacts with local news channels and publications. If you are a student, you could enlist the help of classmates, family, and friends to spread the word about your social impact product to the stakeholders important to your cause. Let's now cover what constitutes a good PR strategy.

Characteristics of a Good PR Strategy

▶ **Its messaging is succinct yet comprehensive.** Reporters, bloggers, and influencers usually have quick turnaround timelines to write a story. Help them by keeping your communications and press releases (which are covered in the following pages) crisp, substantive, and easy to understand.

▶ **It ensures the information you communicate is fact checked.** Ensure your organization's legal, research and development (R&D), marketing, and other relevant functions have confirmed that all data points and facts you plan to communicate in your press releases, press conferences, and interviews are accurate.

▶ **It contains both proactive and reactive messaging strategies**. A *proactive* strategy is the development of an outreach effort to share information with key stakeholders. A *reactive* strategy is the preparation of a protocol and key messages to share only in case a reporter asks or in case of a crisis. A good PR strategy contains both.

If you are ready to share the impact your organization is making in the world, let's dive into the four steps you can take to create your PR strategy.

Step 1: Develop a Key Messages document.

A *Key Messages* document is an internal document a company creates to organize information it eventually wants to share with the public. This document becomes a resource to build press releases from, and it can also be used as a resource to prepare a company's leaders for interviews and speaking engagements. Therefore, effort should be taken to check the messages in this document for accuracy and cultural sensitivity. Exhibit 9.1 shows an example of a Key Messages document for a community center that is preparing to share information about the efforts it is taking to serve its neighbors during the COVID-19 pandemic.

EXHIBIT 9.1 A Key Messages Document for a Community Center

Start with your organi-
zation's purpose, why it
exists.*

Then organize your
thoughts into key themes.

* A great resource for
additional reading on why
it's important to first tell
people about your purpose
is Simon Sinek's book,
Start with Why.

Key Messages

Since 2005, the Green Meadows Community Center has served the needs of its neighbors by listening, advocating, and providing programming that uplifts the community. While still in the midst of the COVID-19 crisis, the community knows it can turn to Green Meadows to provide fresh food, a friendly face, and to listen to what the neighbors need. Here are some of the actions we are currently taking:

Food Access

▶ **The Weekly Food Distribution Program** has grown:
- We are now distributing ~23,000 pounds per month to 1,500 individuals (as reported for June 2020) versus the ~10,000 pounds per month pre-COVID-19 for 175 individuals (average from Oct. 2019–end of Feb. 2020). This includes the 35-pound produce bags that have been created and delivered weekly from church volunteers.
  - ◇ Each family receives 1 weeks' worth of fresh and shelf stable food, tailored to the size of their household. This includes breakfast, lunch, dinner, and snacks for each person of the household per day.
  - ◇ During COVID-19, this program has been expanded to be open to anyone who comes by, and no registration is required
  - ◇ The program happens every Thursday from 11:30 a.m. to 2:00 p.m. while supplies last

▶ **A new One Dish Hot Meal** program has launched:
- This is a meal (like a lasagna or a casserole) that can be eaten that day or frozen and reheated, and feeds a family of ~ 8 people
- The program happens every Friday from 3:00–4:00 p.m.

▶ **COVID-19 Safety Precautions** are being addressed:
- A drive-up has been set up so groceries can be directly loaded into cars
- For neighbors without vehicle access:
  - ◇ A system is set up for walk-ups (this also helps our homeless population). Volunteers will help drop bags at neighbors' homes so they do not have to carry the bags in the heat
  - ◇ We are partnering with Amazon to deliver groceries to those who are high-risk

- We are partnering with the local school district's **School Year and Summer Feeding Program**. They bring their mobile unit to our campus once a week to distribute meals to ~100 students.

Pre-K and After School Elementary Education

- For Pre-K, the **transition from in-person to virtual teaching** began in March
  - As part of our holistic approach, diapers and wipes were mailed to every family in the program when the teaching went virtual
  - The restart is being planned per federal/state/local guidelines for mid-August, with revised health and safety protocols to ensure strict sanitation
  - **On-site precautions** include opening at half capacity, maintaining a 6-foot distance between baby beds and cots, wearing of masks and gloves by teachers, and outdoor playtime will happen in small groups
  - For the families who will continue the program **at home, parents are being equipped to be the child's first teacher.** Parenting videos of the research-based curriculum will be shared via an app.
- For the elementary after-school tutoring program, we are waiting to decide next steps per the school district's schedule and guidelines
- **Internet and technology access are continuing concerns** to keep the kids connected. We are working on securing tablets and hotspots for families to check out.

Community Empowerment and Employment

- We are currently working on the logistics for bringing in a mobile COVID-19 testing unit
- Given recent donor & foundation engagement, we have been able to **hire four members from the community** to help with food distribution programs. These members were affected by the food and restaurant industry layoffs and live within walking distance of our center.

How to Help

- **Community Leaders, Elected Officials, and Media** can help by driving awareness of the issues and opportunities in our community. For example:
  - Showcasing our food expansion efforts and education pivots can help us drive more awareness with our neighbors.
  - Highlighting the lack of internet access and how it affects virtual learning can help us reach potential partners.

> ► **Donors and Volunteers** can help (while taking safety precautions) by:
>
> - Making financial donations on our website: www.xxx.org
> - Donating gift cards help our residents pay rent and phone bills. Please call us ahead of coming in so that we can have someone on-site to receive your donation.
> - Volunteering to put together activity kits for children in the education program. Contact us at contact@xxx.org if you are interested.
>
> While COVID-19 has spotlighted the inequities our neighbors have faced for decades, the community is stepping up its efforts to help overcome them. Green Meadows continues to be a trusted partner for platforms and programs to come in and organize efforts for the highest impact.

With this example as inspiration, draft a Key Messages document about news you would like to share about your social impact organization.

EXERCISE 9.1 Draft a Key Messages Document for Your Social Impact Organization

Key Messages *green ocean initiative*

The Reason Your Organization Exists

The Green Ocean Initiative was created to address the need for the preservation and sustainable development of coastal ecosystems. Our organization is built upon the fact that coastal regions face escalating environmental challenges, including habitat loss, pollution, and climate change impacts.

Theme 1—Key Points *ecosystem preservation and restoration*

▸ Focus on the sustainable management, conservation, and restoration of coastal ecosystems.

▸ We are dedicated to preserving the rich biodiversity of coastal areas by implementing science-based approaches to ecosystem management

▸ Through habitat protection, restoration projects, and sustainable practices we will work on ensuring the long term health of coastal ecosystems

Theme 2—Key Points community empowerment for resilience

▸ Empowering coastal communities through education

▸ We acknowledge the partnership between the health of coastal communities and well-being of the ecosystems around them.

▸ We foster community-led iniatives, providing educational resources, and encouraging sustainable livelihoods, we empower coastal residents to adapt in the face of changes

Theme 3—Key Points Innovation and technology for sustain ability

▸ using innovation and technology to address environmental changes and promote sustainable practices.

▸ We embrace solutions to address the complex environmental issues facing coastal regions.

▸ We use technological innovations for monitering and conservation and community engagement through digital platforms to create effective solutions for sustainable coastal development.

Step 2: Create a press kit.

After creating the foundational Key Messages document, you can now begin pulling together elements of a press kit. Here's roughly what happens to bring a story to life: The press distills information they read in a press release or hear at a press conference, they check this information for accuracy, they get comments and reactions from other sources, and then they report their story. With the tight deadlines and quick turnaround times the press has to manage, the role of a press kit is to make reporting of your story as easy as possible. A press kit can contain elements like:

▸ A press release that contains information in a written document that an organization hopes news outlets will pick up and report

▸ A Frequently Asked Questions document

- Relevant research reports and data points

- Assets like high resolution logos, videos and photos that can be downloaded, approved for use by the press

- Links to an organization's social media sites

- Links to other news stories published about the organization

- Contact information of who the press could reach out to if they want more information or interviews

Let's start putting your press kit together, beginning with a press release. Press releases do not need to be lengthy. The goal is to share just the right amount of information (mainly from your Key Messages document) to interest a reporter in writing about your news. Review the two example press releases in Exhibits 9.2 and 9.3.

EXHIBIT 9.2   Example Press Release with Key Messages for a Fundraising Walk

Press Release

March 15, 2021—To raise funds for cancer research, Company A's annual 5k fundraiser will be held on April 10, 2021 at Memorial Park. Cancer survivors, friends and family walking in honor of those lost, and supporters of all ages are welcome. Kickoff will be at 9 a.m. Distinguished guests will include the mayor and Celebrity X. We'll have live music from Band Y and celebratory drinks and food at the finish line.

Our hope is to raise $1 million for a new cancer research center in the city hospital.

Please register here: www.siteurl.org

For more information, contact Miguel Rodriguez at miguel@nonprofitname.org

Web icon: © Martial Red/Shutterstock.com; Facebook icon: © rvlsoft/Shutterstock.com; Instagram icon: © tanuha2001/Shutterstock.com

Note how this press release includes key messages and information on:

- ► WHERE the event will be
- ► WHEN it will be
- ► WHO is coming (including the target audience, celebrities, etc.)
- ► HOW to register
- ► GOALS and OUTCOMES desired for the event

EXHIBIT 9.3 Example Press Release with Key Messages for a New Product or Service Launch

---

Press Release

January 12, 2021—At Company B we believe that safe drinking water is a fundamental human right. Therefore, today we are launching Product X, which is designed to test and treat water so people in rural communities have safe drinking water. The product is made with recycled material, can be purchased for $5, is very easy to use, and works within 10 minutes.

Product X can be ordered online in bulk for numerous households in a village community. The product can also be ordered to be donated.

This product was developed in partnership with NGO XYZ. Our goal is to distribute this product to 1 million households in Southeast Asia and Africa in year one of this launch and ultimately decrease the number of deaths due to water-borne diseases.

For more information, contact Sophia Cruz at sophia@product.com

---

Note how this press release includes key messages and information on:

► HOW the product works (basic product features and their benefits)

► WHO it is intended to help

► WHERE it can be accessed and used

► WHEN it is available

► GOALS, OUTCOMES, and IMPACT desired

In Exercise 9.2 try to create a press release for news you want to share about your social impact organization.

EXERCISE 9.2   Write a Press Release with Key Messages for Your Organization

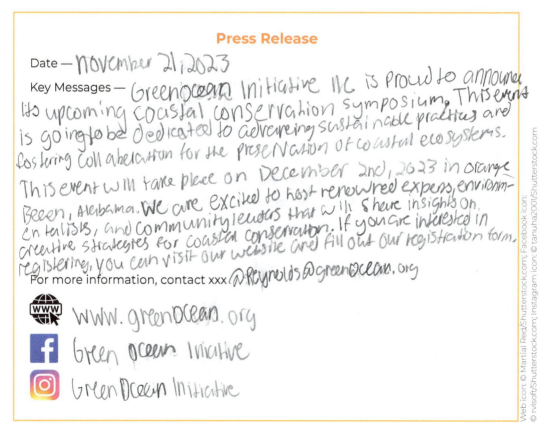

Press Release

Date — november 21, 2023

Key Messages — GreenOcean Initiative INC is proud to announce its upcoming coastal conservation symposium. This event is going to be dedicated to advancing sustainable practices and fostering collaboration for the preservation of coastal ecosystems. This event will take place on December 2nd, 2023 in Orange Beach, Alabama. We are excited to host renowned experts, environmentalists, and community leaders that will share insights on creative strategies for coastal conservation. If you are interested in registering, you can visit our website and fill out our registration form.

For more information, contact xxx @Reynolds@greenocean.org

🌐 www.greenocean.org

f Green Ocean Initiative

📷 GreenOcean Initiative

For advanced writers who want to make a press release more compelling, try applying the flow of a ***master narrative*** that describes a social innovation's ***theory of change.*** (The theory of change framework is used by social innovators to explain their belief in how certain activities will lead to the outputs, outcomes, and change they hope to see in the world.)

EXHIBIT 9.4 Master Narrative Framework

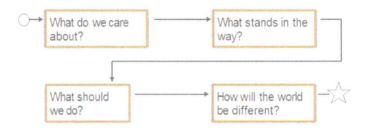

This is the Master Narrative Framework Sandy Skees, EVP/Global Lead Purpose & Impact Practice at Porter Novelli, a global Purpose-based Communications Consultancy, uses to train her team.

After completing your press release, let's look at creating a Frequently Asked Questions document. This is a pretty simple but extremely helpful document that can contain information that doesn't necessarily fit in a Key Messages document. Reporters might be able to find answers in this document to questions they didn't have time to cover during an interview. An organization's board or staff member might also refer to this document prior to an interview to refresh their memory on certain pieces of information.

EXHIBIT 9.5   A Frequently Asked Questions Document for a Sustainable Chocolate Product Sold by a Nonprofit That Employs Refugee Women

---

Frequently Asked Questions

Q: How do we know the new product is safe to eat?

A: The product has been certified by _____ government organization and _____ a 3rd party verifying body.

Q: Does the new product employ Fair Trade labor practices?

A: Yes, all our tradesmen get paid a living wage.

Q: Is the product made with organic ingredients?

A: Yes, and the ingredients (sugar and cocoa) are certified organic by x organization.

Q: Is the product's packaging recyclable?

A: Yes.

Q: Who should we contact for more information?

A: contact@companyname.org

Try to recall the questions you've received most often about your social impact idea. Capture those questions and their corresponding answers in Exercise 9.3.

Frequently Asked Questions

Q: What projects does GreenOcean initiative llc participate in for coastal conservation?

A: We engage in many different projects, like marine biodiversity, habitat restoration, and community development initiatives. We focus on giving back to the environment and local communities.

Q: How can people get involved in our organization?

A: People can get involved by volunteering, donating, or even participating in educational programs.

Q: How does our organization measure the success of its conservation efforts?

A: We employ a mix of community feedback, environmental indicators, and scientific monitoring to measure the success of our projects.

Q: What sets GreenOcean apart from other organizations?

A: We stand out because of our unique approach combining environmental conservation, technological innovation, and community assent.

Q: How does GreenOcean address the impact of climate change on coastal regions?

A: We use different strategies like land-use planning and community education on climate related risks and problems. We encourage communities to adapt.

> **Q:** Can other businesses partner with Green Ocean?
>
> **A:** Yes! We love partnering with other businesses that are also interested in supporting sustainable coastal initiatives.
>
> **Q:** How can I stay in the know about Green Ocean Iniative?
>
> **A:** Our website and social media accounts are the best way to stay in the know as we share updates on projects, events, and even opportunities for involvement.

Once you've crafted your press release and Frequently Asked Questions document, all you need to do to complete your press kit is to collate the other pieces of information you think could be helpful to someone reporting on your organization (like high resolution logos and photos that are approved for use and can accompany the story).

Step 3: Create a communications outreach plan and timeline.

Now that you've taken the effort to create a press kit, let's think through all the different channels you could send it to. In Exercise 9.4 list the names of channels and publications you'd like to see your story reported in. Then list the contacts you have at those news outlets. If you don't have any contacts in these outlets yet, search for reporters' contact information on the internet or ask your teammates and board members if they have any connections.

EXERCISE 9.4 Create a List of Media Contacts by Channel

Channel (includes Owned, Earned, and Paid Media*)	Specific Name of News Channel or Publication	Contact Name, Email Address or Phone Number
Online: Email Newsletters, Blogs, Social Media, and Influencers	1. 2. 3.	1. 2. 3.
TV: Local News Stations, National News Stations, and Specific News Programs	1. 2. 3.	1. 2. 3.

Print—Magazines, Newspapers	1.	1.
	2.	2.
	3.	3.
Radio—Local/ national radio channels, Podcasts	1.	1.
	2.	2.
	3.	3.

*Owned media are a brand's marketing channels that it manages itself—its social media accounts, its own blog, and its own email newsletters. Earned media is reporting about your brand or organization by journalists, without payment from the brand. Paid media is a media placement that a brand pays for via sponsorship or advertising fees.

Once you have the chart in Exercise 9.4 filled out, create a communications timeline of when to reach out to the different media channels, but also think more broadly. Besides engaging with the media, there are other ways to share your message. In Exhibit 9.6 you will see media outreach is only in one box, illustrating that PR efforts include outreach to a broader list of stakeholders.

EXHIBIT 9.6 A Communications Timeline for a Community Center's Holiday Party

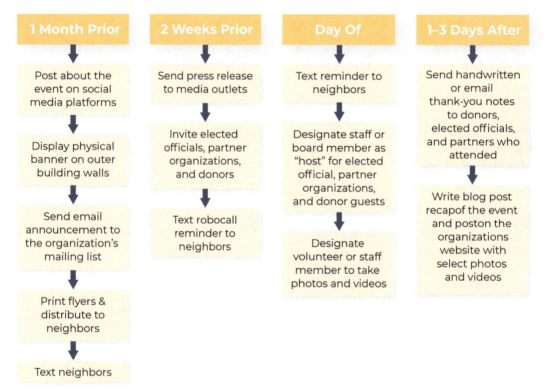

1 Month Prior	2 Weeks Prior	Day Of	1–3 Days After
Post about the event on social media platforms	Send press release to media outlets	Text reminder to neighbors	Send handwritten or email thank-you notes to donors, elected officials, and partners who attended
Display physical banner on outer building walls	Invite elected officials, partner organizations, and donors	Designate staff or board member as "host" for elected official, partner organizations, and donor guests	Write blog post recapof the event and poston the organizations website with select photos and videos
Send email announcement to the organization's mailing list	Text robocall reminder to neighbors	Designate volunteer or staff member to take photos and videos	
Print flyers & distribute to neighbors			
Text neighbors			

Give it a try and create a communications timeline for your own organization.

EXERCISE 9.5 Create a Communications Timeline of When to Reach out to Key Stakeholders for a Key Event

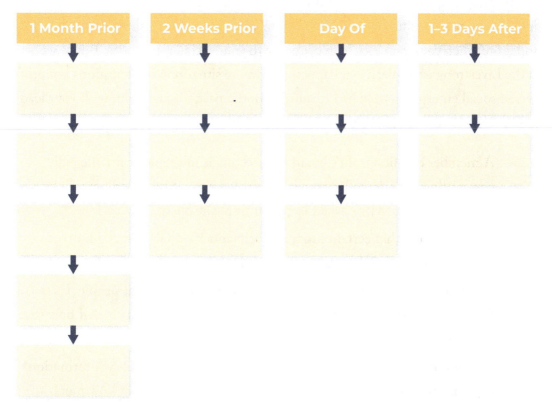

1 Month Prior	2 Weeks Prior	Day Of	1–3 Days After

If you completed the three steps, you are now ready to combine your press release, Frequently Asked Questions document, and other relevant materials into a press kit to send to the media. You or your PR teammate can email this press kit directly to reporters you know. If you don't know specific reporters, press releases (with links to their comprehensive press kits) can be shared via platforms like PRnewswire.com or CSRwire.com and/or on your organization's website.

Step 4: Develop a reactive *PR strategy.*

In this final step, you will prepare for how to handle communications during a tough, unforeseen, or crisis situation. It is hard to imagine that your organization could come under fire when your goal is to help people with your social impact idea. But as we saw in the Livestrong example, it can happen. Below are situations and questions nonprofits and social enterprises have had to address in the past; discuss them with your leadership team so you can plan for how your organization might approach them:

- A member of a nonprofit's board of directors is in the news for allegedly committing a white-collar crime; stakeholders ask if that member will be suspended, removed, or asked to resign from the board.

- It is uncovered that certain program recipients have falsified eligibility requirements. Other program recipients have learned of this and are upset.

- Social media posts have unintentionally offended a group of people. Even though the post is removed, the media still wants an explanation of how that happened.

- A nonprofit pays a market-competitive salary (nonprofit salary information often is accessible to the public), but donors become upset at how much employees are paid as some feel that nonprofit salaries should not be as high as corporate salaries.

- An organization's spending on events is deemed exorbitant.

Discussing these scenarios with your leadership team ahead of time, when you aren't in crisis mode, can help you respond quickly when needed. How you react and what you say in a crisis will reflect the values of your organization. If donors and investors feel like an organization isn't staying true to its mission or values, donation dollars can come under jeopardy.

Use the following template to have this dialogue with your leadership team. Fill out the worksheet in Exercise 9.6 and keep it on file in case a crisis occurs. (You can reproduce the worksheet with questions that are pertinent to your organization.)

EXERCISE 9.6 Create a Reactive Media Strategy

Reactive PR Strategy & Messaging

This should not be shared with the media but kept on file by the organization's leadership team.

The questions below can be used for reference if or when a crisis occurs, so that the leadership team can be timely in its response and holistic in its approach in managing a situation in accordance with the organization's values.

1. How will we respond if an accident happens on our premises?

2. How will we respond if asked about a new policy or legislation being considered by the government that does not have bipartisan support but is connected to our work?

3. How will we respond if a leader, board member, large investor, large donor, or staff member is caught in a scandal?

4. What will we do if our system is hacked or we have a loss of data?

5. How will we respond if we are accused of discriminatory practices?

6. How will we communicate with our stakeholders if a crisis occurs? Will we send an email, text, or will our CEO make personal phone calls?

In addition to discussing these questions with your team before a crisis occurs, it's also wise to have a cross-functional crisis management team designated if one indeed occurs. Current events and the political climate should be considered when handling a delicate situation. The wisdom and judgment of a trusted group of advisors who can be brought together quickly to discuss an appropriate plan of action could prove invaluable. This group of advisors could include members of your organization's internal leadership team as well as leaders external to your organization. It is also helpful to have on hand names of organizations you have partnered with, or beneficiaries of your services, who would be open to speaking positively about your organization if needed. Fill out the template below with their names and contact information.

EXERCISE 9.7   Fill out These Crisis Management Templates for Your Organization

Crisis Management Team

This is the team to quickly gather when a crisis occurs, and a response is required from the organization. All teammates' perspectives must be gathered to provide a response that is timely, sensitive, and holistic.

Function	Name and Phone Number
Executive Director	
Community Relations	
PR/Marketing	
Legal	
Finance	
Partner Organizations	

Supporters

Key partner organizations that will be supportive in a crisis situation and could be open to speaking publicly and positively about our organization:

1.

2.

Key individuals (program recipients, customers, or donors) who can be called to speak positively about our impact:

1.

2.

3.

4.

5.

These documents should only be shared with your organization's leadership team and are not to be shared with the media.

To end this chapter on a lighter note, all mistakes or blunders need not be addressed in a serious fashion. Here's an example of what happened at the American Red Cross. At a happy hour, someone managing the American Red Cross Twitter account posted this:

The American Red Cross addressed the situation and handled it with humor. On its blog, the American Red Cross thanked its supporters for being understanding and used the accident to encourage donations:

> *We found so many of you to be sympathetic and understanding. While we're a 130 year old humanitarian organization, we're also made up of human beings. Thanks for not only getting that but for turning our faux pas into something good. You immediately embraced this mix-up and many of you have pledged donations to the Red Cross.*

Wendy Harman, social media director for the Red Cross explained, *"We are an organization that deals with life-changing disasters and this wasn't one of them. It was just a little mistake."*

Even with the best of intentions, humans make mistakes, and consumers can appreciate some humanity and humor. All PR incidents aren't as dramatic as the Livestrong scandal.

CONNECTING THE DOTS

Confirm that you are sharing your PR news on your owned channels—like on the website you built in Chapter 6 and on the social media sites you developed in Chapter 8. Go back a few more chapters—did you communicate the details about your 5 P's from Chapter 1 in your key messages?
Does your PR plan include customized outreach to all the consumers, customers, company associates, and collaborators you outlined in Chapter 2?

PART 3

EVALUATE

In Part 3 of this guidebook you will learn how to measure the impact of the work you did in Parts 1 and 2. While there is only one chapter in this section, it is a significant one. Analyzing which of your marketing tactics are working well (and which ones could be improved) can help you focus your efforts toward what can effectively drive change.

CHAPTER 10

Measuring Success: How to Value Your Marketing's Impact

Here we are at the final chapter. We've covered the fundamentals of what is required to bring a social impact idea to market. But we're not done. Perhaps the most important question comes up now: Did the time, money, and effort we invested in Chapters 1–9 prove fruitful? What marketing tactics are working well and where might we pivot? These are the questions you, your team, your manager, and/or your board of directors will want answered.

To illustrate the complexity of trying to answer these questions, try to remember the last time you decided to donate to a cause, buy a product that had a social impact, or volunteer with an organization. What convinced you to do it?

▸ Did you see a *social media post* your friend Liked about an organization's upcoming event?

▸ Did you get an *email* at work saying your company has a volunteer day with the organization?

▸ Did you see in a *shop window* that a percentage of a certain product's sales will benefit the organization?

- Did you see a *news report* about a hurricane and then see an ad for the organization's disaster relief efforts?

- Was the *time of year* Christmas, Hanukkah, Eid, Diwali or another holiday when you received a mailer from the organization and felt especially in the giving spirit?

It is likely that multiple marketing efforts (also known as tactics or activations) influenced how you engaged with that social impact organization. Instead of a singular social media post, email, billboard, ad, or time of year driving your behavior, it was likely some combination of these.

This ambiguity makes attributing the effectiveness of individual marketing tactics difficult. But if you enjoyed the work in Chapters 1–9 and have a feeling that your marketing efforts are working, you may want to understand and quantify its effectiveness for two main reasons:

- **It creates benchmarks for future campaigns.** By analyzing the results of your marketing activities against the time and resources you put into them, you will have a rough guide of what type of investment would be required to attain similar results in the future.

- **It can help secure additional funding.** Having data points to prove the effectiveness of your marketing helps in conversations with your funders. Funders can be a nonprofit's donors, a corporate finance department, or your organization's leadership team. They will want to know whether the time and money you spent on marketing delivered growth for the organization before they set aside funds for additional marketing expenses.

With this understanding of how valuable measurement is, let's discuss another challenge: time. Social impact marketing has a longer timeline than traditional marketing. In traditional marketing, a sale could happen within a week of consumers seeing a promotion. Brand managers typically run weekly reports to see how their brand performed. They might look at metrics like the total number of units sold, the average price point of the units sold, and how many incremental in-store displays were secured with a promotion or campaign.

With social impact marketing though, impact may not be realized for several months or even years. For example, let's say you develop a fortified snack that is intended to help children in developing countries get the vitamins and nutrients they need. You can quantify the number of snacks you are able to sell, but the resulting impact on children's nutrition scores will take months to realize. Moreover, it will require partnership with doctors' offices and the healthcare system which takes time to organize, especially when patient privacy is a priority. Here's another example. Let's say a new policy is enacted to incentivize manufacturers to use renewable energy. While manufacturers may want to use this incentive, renewable energy resources must be available, affordable, and implementable at the scale required to run large manufacturing sites. It can take months or years before the impact on air quality from this policy can be realized.

The timeline for measuring marketing's impact is a challenge for everyone. If you are a student helping a nonprofit, it's likely you might not see the results of your social impact marketing before the semester is over. If you work at a corporation, you might move on to another project before the results of your social impact marketing campaigns are realized. If you work at a nonprofit, it may be hard to secure a grant for a measurement study that lasts multiple years.

While time and measurement are a challenge, when results are realized, they can show up in unexpected and beautiful ways. In September 2017, Dallas Heroes Project (DHP), an organization with a mission to create marketing campaigns that amplify the work of local heroes, launched a campaign featuring Dale Long. Dale had been mentoring young men through the Big Brothers Big Sisters organization for over 43 years and had a message for the city of Dallas: it needed more African American male mentors.

With the goal of inspiring more African American men to volunteer with Big Brothers Big Sisters, DHP launched a month-long 360 degree activation campaign with Dale at the center. The campaign included print and digital articles and short videos of Dale that were shared across social media. With the analytic capabilities of social media, DHP was able to target its media dollars to specific audiences of alumni and members of historically Black colleges and universities (HBCUs) and the Alpha Phi Alpha fraternity (the first intercollegiate fraternity established for African American men) in the Dallas-Fort Worth metroplex. Partners from Dale's church and office enthusiastically shared the videos and articles as well through their email and social media channels.

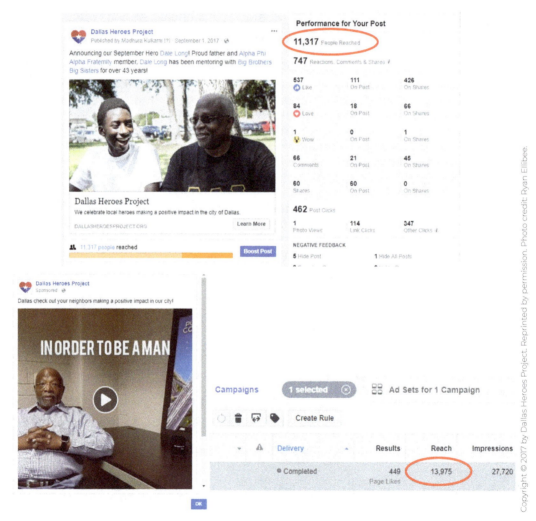

During the campaign, DHP checked in with Big Brothers Big Sisters to see if the marketing efforts were having an effect in the number of new mentors signing up. But the organization did not report any significant upticks in enrollment. A few months later, however, on December 14, *Dallas Morning News,* the city's prominent newspaper, ran a story: "*This is what Dallas needs: Nearly 600 men answer the call to mentor South Dallas students.*"

Here's what happened: Dade Middle School was having a Breakfast with Dads event and the organizers needed male mentors for the young boys who did not have a father figure in their lives. The organizers sent out the request as they traditionally would via social media, email, and word of mouth. The surprising result was that they needed about 50 mentors, and *600 showed up!* Six hundred men essentially answered the call to action and said, "Yes, we are here for you. We care about you and your future." Can you imagine how happy and excited those young boys must have felt?

Was it a coincidence that, after decades of a shortage of male mentors, an event brought together over 10 times the number of volunteers needed? And that being just three and a half months after DHP ran its campaign on Dale? It's hard to say for sure, but it felt like a victory for the team at DHP, it felt like a victory for all the people who were sharing Dale's message, and it felt like a victory for the Dallas community.

The team at DHP initially completed their evaluation report one month after they ended their campaign. After this news at Dade Middle School though, they updated their report. While enrollment in the Big Brothers Big Sisters program didn't necessarily see an uptick in enrollment immediately, mentoring within the city rose and the overarching social impact goal was achieved. With this case as inspiration, let's now study what a comprehensive marketing evaluation looks like.

Characteristics of a Thorough Marketing Effectiveness Evaluation

▶ **The analysis should include both qualitative and quantitative data.** (Refer to Chapter 4 to review the differences between qualitative and quantitative data.) In your evaluation reports, quantitative data can provide credibility and qualitative data can provide color. For example, if you are reporting on a female farmer empowerment program in a developing country, quantitative data can show how the program helped increase female farmer crop yields and conserve water with drip irrigation practices. It can demonstrate how much money female farmers were able to earn and put into a savings account. But adding in qualitative data to the report can also reveal how female farmers feel more respected from their husbands and in-laws as a result of the program. This helps paint a more comprehensive picture of the program's impact. (Unfortunately, these programs have caused instances of domestic violence against female farmers due to the changes in gender norms within the family unit. These stories should be reported on as well so preventative measures can be taken.)

► **The evaluation should stay focused on measuring progress against all three social impact marketing goals.** Remember the three main goals in social impact marketing: building brand equity, increasing sales, and creating positive impact. Also remember from our conversation on goals and key performance indicators in Chapter 7 that for this book's purposes we will expand how we define these three goals. We will expand "build brand equity" to include "build awareness." Because unless there is a scandal or a bad product experience, in most instances brand equity increases with awareness-driving initiatives. And since social impact marketing causes may not have a specific product at the heart of its idea, we will expand "sales" to include "engagements." Case in point, if a social impact goal is for rural women's financial empowerment, then instead of a product sale, we'd want to count the number of women who engage in a job training program. Finally, we will expand our "positive impact" goal to include "positive behavior change." For example, if our goal is to reduce hate speech on social media, that will require people to change their behavior online. Therefore, our three goals become:

1. Building brand equity or awareness
2. Increasing sales or engagements
3. Creating positive impact or positive behavior change

It is important for social impact marketing efforts to address all three goals, else the impact remains incomplete. For instance, if a campaign gets substantial media attention and pulls at the heartstrings but doesn't offer meaningful and concrete actions for positive change, the campaign falls short of creating a positive impact; it hasn't gone far enough. On the other hand, if a campaign tries to get people to change behavior or adopt a new policy without spending time driving awareness and engagement around an issue, it is unlikely to get support.

In general, a lot of activities are needed (via a 360 degree campaign) to drive awareness and understanding of a product or cause before people will engage with it. Eventually, engagement with your product or cause will drive behavior change and lead to the positive impact you wish to create.

EXHIBIT 10.1 3 Tiers of Marketing Goals

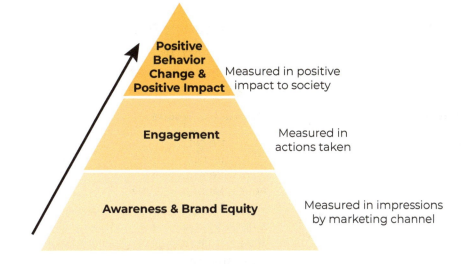

▶ **All tactics in a 360 degree marketing campaign should be analyzed to determine their return on investment.** Some marketing activities require a low investment of time or money but can potentially have a huge return. Or some marketing tactics could require a large investment of time and money but have little return. It's important to do an audit of all the activities you try so you know where you want to invest in the future.

Let's now start pulling your evaluation plan together. We'll start with simple steps before getting into a more complex analysis.

Step 1: Start with simply listing key qualitative and quantitative learnings from your marketing efforts.

An easy place to begin your evaluation is by reflecting on any "aha's" you experienced with your 360 degree campaign activation. Think through what surprised you (good or bad) and what made you proud. Think through what learnings could influence future marketing activations.

EXHIBIT 10.2 Key Learnings from a Restaurant That Equips At-Risk Youth with Life Skills & Employment Opportunities

Key Learnings	
Quantitative Results	**Qualitative Results**
80% of young adults that go through our internships avoid recidivism.	Corporate catering events are enjoyed by our interns since they get to meet professionals from different industries and learn about different career opportunities.
Our short videos on social media get five times more views and engagements than our static photos.	The local newspaper awarded us the "Sustainability Champion" designation because of our sustainability & food waste diversion efforts. This generated positive press for our restaurant.
Our online reservations went up 25% when we joined a new digital reservations platform.	Adding a rooftop herb garden at the restaurant has increased its ambiance and interns enjoy taking care of it.

With Exhibit 10.2 as an example, fill out the chart in Exercise 10.1.

EXERCISE 10.1 Capture Key Learnings from Your Marketing Activities

Key Learnings	
Quantitative Results	**Qualitative Results**

Step 2: Decide on the KPIs for each of your three social impact marketing goals.

The topic of key performance indicators was introduced in Chapter 7 in the context of determining how you measure the success of a campaign. Here in Chapter 10, consider KPIs for a broader time frame and scope, perhaps a year's time frame for a whole set of marketing activities including multiple campaigns, your website, social media, and PR efforts.

Exhibit 10.3 lists a sample of KPIs for each of our three social impact marketing goals. In general, positive impact goals should be very high-level goals that transcend beyond the success of your organization. Engagement and sales goals are benchmarks to track your organization's individual success in driving a specific consumer action that has direct influence on achieving the positive impact goals. And awareness and brand equity goals exist so you can generate consumer understanding and familiarity about your brand and the cause you work on.

EXHIBIT 10.3 Sample Key Performance Indicators per Marketing Goal

Key Performance Indicators		
Positive Impact & Behavior Change Goals	**Engagement & Sales Goals**	**Awareness & Brand Equity Goals**
Poverty: ▶ Increase in the number of people earning a living wage Hunger: ▶ Decrease in the number of people relying on government food subsidies Health: ▶ Increase in the number of cancer survivors ▶ Decrease in the number of suicides and depression cases Education: ▶ Increase in the number of girls getting access to education Clean Water: ▶ Increase in the number of people with convenient access to clean drinking water Climate: ▶ More plastic is recycled ▶ Less plastic ends up in the ocean ▶ More agricultural land is developed in a regenerative way	Donations: ▶ Total amount of donations (Did you reach your fundraising goal?) ▶ Average value of donations (How much do your target consumers/donors like to donate to your cause?) ▶ Number of repeat donors (Are you keeping your donors engaged?) Volunteers: ▶ Number of volunteers (Are you able to secure the number of volunteers you need?) ▶ Number of repeat volunteers (Do your volunteers have fun and feel like they make an impact, and thus want to keep coming back?) Partnerships: ▶ Number of collaborators who help you (Indicates if your organization is easy to work with)	Website: ▶ Number of people visiting your organization's website per week or per month Social Media: ▶ Number of people Liking or Following your page ▶ Number of people Viewing/Liking/Hearting/Sharing your posts Print: ▶ Number of households/circulations the print medium (newspaper, magazine, or flyer) reaches Radio/Podcasts: ▶ Number of radio channels/podcasts playing your ad or inviting you to speak on their show ▶ Number of listeners per radio channel/podcast you reach with your ad or interview TV: ▶ Number of people who see your ad

Positive Impact & Behavior Change Goals	Engagement & Sales Goals	Awareness & Brand Equity Goals
(This space is blank since the list of marketing actions in the other two columns should be longer than the list of goals you are trying to achieve.)	Activations: ▶ Number of people who sign up and attend an event (like a 5k walk) ▶ Number of people who sign a petition ▶ Number of people who host a fundraiser Sales: ▶ Dollar and unit sales ▶ Velocities (how many units sold in one week) ▶ Distribution (how many retail outlets sell your product)	Online video: ▶ Number of partial video views ▶ Number of full video views ▶ Number of repeat video views Email: ▶ Number of people on your email list serve ▶ Number of people who open one of your emails ▶ Number of people who click on links within an email Public Relations: ▶ Number of positive or negative PR mentions ▶ Number of organizations that reach out to you given your PR outreach ▶ Number of impressions your brand ambassadors or hired social media influencers garner Brand Equity: ▶ After seeing the campaign, how do people score the brand on metrics like increased purchase intent, brand favorability, brand awareness, credibility and shareability (i.e. would people share the campaign with their friends?)

The next two exhibits show which KPIs were chosen by two different organizations. Notice the similarities and differences between them given the nature of their work.

EXHIBIT 10.4   Marketing KPIs for a Homeless Shelter

Key Performance Indicators		
Positive Impact & Behavior Change Goals	**Engagement & Sales Goals**	**Awareness & Brand Equity Goals**
▶ There is a decrease in the average number of days people stay at the shelter given our services help them find more permanent options ▶ There is an increase in the number of people who find living wage employment by the time they leave the shelter ▶ The shelter can operate at full capacity when needed, and can refer people to other shelters when they have reached capacity	Donations: ▶ Total amount of monetary donations ▶ Average value of monetary donations ▶ Number of repeat donors ▶ Number of in-kind donations like blankets, jackets, toiletries Volunteers: ▶ How many volunteers come to serve or prepare meals? ▶ Number of repeat volunteers Partnerships: ▶ Number of job placement agencies and food pantries that partner with the shelter Activations: ▶ Number of people at the shelter who attend a resume review and interview prep workshop	Website: ▶ Number of people visiting the organization's website per week or per month Social Media: ▶ Number of people Liking or Following the organization's page ▶ Number of people Viewing/Liking/Hearting/Sharing the organization's posts Print: ▶ Number of households/circulations the print medium (newspaper, magazine, or flyer) reaches Radio/Podcasts: ▶ Number of radio channels/podcasts playing your ad or inviting you to speak on their show ▶ Number of listeners per radio channel/podcast you reach with your ad or interview

Positive Impact & Behavior Change Goals	Engagement & Sales Goals	Awareness & Brand Equity Goals
		Email: ▶ Number of people on the organization's email list ▶ Number of people who open one of the organization's emails ▶ Number of people who click on links within an email Public Relations: ▶ Number of positive or negative PR mentions ▶ Number of organizations that reach out with a speaking invitation to share information about the homeless shelter with a house of worship, workplace, or social group

EXHIBIT 10.5 Marketing KPIs for an Organization That Helps Young Women Run for Government Office

Key Performance Indicators		
Positive Impact & Behavior Change Goals	**Engagement & Sales Goals**	**Awareness & Brand Equity Goals**
▸ Increase in the number of women holding elected positions in the government	Donations: ▸ Total amount of monetary donations ▸ Average value of donations ▸ Number of repeat donors ▸ Number of in-kind donations like business suits or transportation funding to visit government offices Volunteers: ▸ Number of volunteers who come to talk to the young women about their experience in government Partnerships: ▸ Number of colleges and universities who partner with the organization to open chapters on their campus ▸ Number of state and national government senators and representatives that provide internships for young women who want to run for office	Website: ▸ Number of people visiting the organization's website per week or per month Social Media: ▸ Number of people Liking or Following the organization's page ▸ Number of people Viewing/Liking/Hearting/Sharing the organization's posts Print: ▸ Number of households/circulations the print medium (newspaper, magazine, or flyer) reaches Radio/Podcasts: ▸ Number of radio channels/podcasts playing your ad or inviting you to speak on their show ▸ Number of listeners per radio channel/podcast you reach with your ad or interview

Positive Impact & Behavior Change Goals	Engagement & Sales Goals	Awareness & Brand Equity Goals
	Political campaigns: ▶ Increase in the number of young women running for government office ▶ Number of people who donate to a specific young woman's political campaign	Email: ▶ Number of people on the organization's email list ▶ Number of people who open one of the organization's emails ▶ Number of people who click on links within an email Public Relations: ▶ Number of positive or negative PR mentions ▶ Number of colleges or university organizations that reach out for someone at the organization to speak at their events

You might have noticed the awareness KPIs are similar in both examples. This is because the channels we use to drive awareness have standardized metrics. The positive impact KPIs and a few of the engagement KPIs are the ones with the variation since they are unique to a specific cause.

Now plan the KPIs for how you will measure positive impact, engagement, and awareness for your social impact idea. While this exercise is in the last chapter of this book, planning KPIs *before* starting your marketing efforts can keep you focused *during* the year on the outcomes you've predetermined to drive.

EXERCISE 10.2   Plan KPIs for Your Marketing Goals

Key Performance Indicators		
Positive Impact & Behavior Change Goals	**Engagement & Sales Goals**	**Awareness & Brand Equity Goals**
What positive change do you want to drive in society with your idea and what metric will increase or decrease if that change happens?	How do you want people to engage in your mission? Do you want them to donate, volunteer, partner, or participate in a certain activity? What data points will you use to measure this?	How will you leverage various marketing channels to drive awareness of your organization, cause, product, or service? What metrics will you analyze to ensure these channels are indeed effective in increasing awareness?

Step 3: Track and analyze your results.

At the end of the year or another set time period (perhaps after six months), capture the results of your marketing activities against the KPIs you set in Exercise 10.2.

EXERCISE 10.3   Report the Results of Your Marketing Efforts

KPI Results		
Positive Impact & Behavior Change Goals	**Engagement & Sales Goals**	**Awareness & Brand Equity Goals**
E.g. What positive change occurred this year?	E.g. How much money was raised for your cause? How many volunteers did you work with? How many people came to your events?	E.g. How many impressions did your social media activities garner? How many listeners were you able to reach with the podcasts you were interviewed on?

Review the results and see if you are happy with these numbers. The success in achieving the KPIs in your Positive Impact column will depend on how effective and efficient your marketing tactics are in the Engagement and Awareness columns. If you think there's room for improvement in engagement rates, think through ways you might reduce barriers to engagement. For instance, if you are trying to get people to sign a petition, assess if it's easy for them to do so. Would it help if you spent some money to create a digital version of the petition? Would it help if you spent some time creating a bilingual option? If you think there's room for improvement in awareness rates, think through how you might better reach your audience. Instead of spending most of your resources on Facebook and Instagram, might you diversify your outreach by being a guest speaker on podcasts that specifically address the cause you work on?

To take this analysis a bit deeper, let's discuss three common terms connected to evaluation and measurement and how they can be used to inform your marketing decisions:

- **Return on Investment (ROI):** ROI is the net financial benefit you receive from an investment divided by the cost of that investment. It can be expressed as a ratio or as a percentage.

- **Social Return on Investment (SROI):** SROI includes accounting for any social or environmental benefits that a traditional financial ROI analysis doesn't capture.

- **Cost-Benefit Analysis:** This analysis compares the resources (like time and money) required to do certain activities to achieve certain benefits. It also considers the cost of not doing a certain activity.

ROI is used to compare similar activations within a channel. For instance, we could compare the effectiveness of Facebook versus Instagram in a promotion we run to raise donations. In a hypothetical situation, let's say we invest $100 on each platform to boost an advertisement that asks people to hit the Donate Now button and make a donation. If we are able to raise $500 on Facebook and $1000 on Instagram, the ROI for each would be calculated as such:

Facebook	
Net Benefit (Benefit – cost)	$500–$100
Net Investment (Cost)	$100
ROI	$400/$100 = 4 or 400%

Instagram	
Net Benefit (Benefit – cost)	$1000–$100
Net Investment (Cost)	$100
ROI	$900/$100 = 9 or 900%

We would articulate this as, "The return on investment from our Facebook ad was 4X, or 400%, while the return on investment from our Instagram ad was 9X or 900%." This result might prompt us to spend more ad dollars on Instagram and less ad dollars on Facebook in the future. It might give an indication that more of our target consumers or target donors are on Instagram. Or it may prompt us to investigate further—perhaps we were able to engage more donors on Facebook but they gave smaller donations than the people who donated through Instagram. If this is the case, we might want to continue spending ad dollars on both platforms to benefit from the reach and depth they provide together.

Social return on investment is an analysis that considers benefits that are hard to quantify but that have a positive impact on people or the environment. For instance, if a company makes an effort to ensure diversity in its advertising, the social return is the promotion of inclusivity within a culture. It might take more time and money to work with agencies on finding diverse models to work with, and it's hard to calculate the impact of one ad on people feeling represented in the media, but we know it's a step in the right direction. Marketers are now finding it a bit easier to start quantifying the social returns of environmental efforts though. If a company decides to launch a product that is environmentally friendly, it can now quantify efforts like how much water it is able to save in its manufacturing processes, how much plastic it is able to divert from landfills if the packaging is biodegradable, and how many trees are being planted to offset its carbon footprint. Marketers can then study and quantify the impact of these efforts on brand equity and sales.

A cost-benefit analysis helps marketers look at all their marketing activities in aggregate and compare them to one another. In this analysis, "costs" include both costs in time and costs in money needed to execute an activation. It also includes considering the cost of not doing an activity (like not having a website would make it difficult for potential program recipients or donors to find you). "Benefits" include both what can be measured quantitatively (like donations and PR impressions) and what can be measured qualitatively (like goodwill generated with partners). Unlike in the ROI analysis where we compared results from our activations within the same channel, in this analysis we will compare activities across all the marketing channels in which we activate. This will make quantifying and comparing results difficult. For example, if we host a volunteer event that costs us $2,000 to run and we benefit from the time of 200 volunteers for three hours and $5,000 in donations, how would we compare that to the effectiveness of spending $100 on a social media ad that reaches 10,000 people and gets 50 people to donate a cumulative $2,500? It is hard to compare the two since the quality of an engagement in a live volunteer event will likely be more impactful to a person long term versus seeing an ad on social media. This illustrates that this type of cost-benefit analysis requires judgment. See the example in Exhibit 10.6 where costs and benefits are assessed more generally than quantitatively as Low, Medium, or High.

EXHIBIT 10.6 Cost-Benefit Analysis for Marketing Activities of a City Food Bank

	Benefits	Costs			Value	Notes
Activities						
		Cost in Money	**Cost in Time**	**Cost of Not Doing the Activity**		
Awareness Activities						
Bi-weekly email newsletter	300 people came to our event after reading the invitation in our emails	Low (we use a free email service)	Medium (about 2 hours per week)	Without email we lose the primary way we communicate with our most engaged consumers	Medium	We will try to make our emails shorter and see if a weekly email cadence results in higher open rates.
Social media	Facebook: $500 donations per month via the Donate Now Button	Medium (since we hire a social media marketing contractor)	Medium (the social media marketer monitors the social media pages daily)	Without an active Facebook page, we lose out on the donations and event sign ups we get through this platform	High	
	Instagram: a few hundred Hearts for each post			Without Instagram we lose our primary method of communicating with our high school and college volunteers	High	We will likely close our Twitter account to focus on Facebook and Instagram. We will try to write more articles on LinkedIn and see if we get consistent engagement there.
	Twitter: 3–5 comments and about 10 Hearts per post			Not much—many people don't expect or need us to be on Twitter	Low	
	LinkedIn: we've only posted 1 article thus far but got about 150 Likes			Not much—many people don't expect or need us to be on LinkedIn (but they do engage with us when we post here)	To be determined	

		Cost in Money	Cost in Time	Cost of Not Doing the Activity		
Podcast interviews	We attract about 2–3 organizational partners when we speak on podcasts + about 20-30 new people who reach out for our services	$0	Low 5 hours per month	Not much—many people don't expect us to be on podcasts (but we get good feedback when we are on them)	High	These are fun to do and we can repost links to them on our social media accounts.
Website refresh	About 15-20 people reach out for our services each month after we refreshed our website. We have about 250 website visitors each month and receive about $1500 in donations each month through our website.	Medium $5000 one time cost to update the site + a few hundred dollars every quarter to make small updates	High for 2 months, then very low investment	There is a high cost for not having a professional looking website. Websites are the first place people go to learn about nonprofits. We also have to include a link to our website in all our grant applications. We need the website to function well to manage volunteer signups and receive donations.	High	We should try to refresh our website every 3-4 years

Engagement Activities

		Cost in Money	Cost in Time	Cost of Not Doing the Activity		
Annual fundraising event	$20,000 donations + PR mentions in 12 publications with a circulation totaling 1.2 million readership + was introduced to new donors		High for 3 months	The biggest loss if we don't do this event is the PR we get from it. But we don't need this event to fundraise.	Medium monetary return High PR return	Our team and our donors look forward to our annual event but we should try a new format to keep costs low.

Activity	Results	Cost	Time	Value	Rating	Notes
Back to School canned food drive	9000 pounds of canned food was donated by elementary school children	Low got the word out through email and outreach to the elementary schools	High only for 3 weeks	Without this event, we lose an easy way to connect with our community and bring people in to see our facilities.	High	Parents were happy to get their children involved in community service. Many of the parents also made monetary donations.
Learning tour of neighborhood food deserts via city bus	To be determined.	Low (only the cost of hiring the bus and driver)	High for 1.5 months to coordinate, Tour lasted only 3 hours	Without this event, it is difficult for our partners to connect with and understand the issues facing our neighbors in food deserts.	To be determined	A few corporate partners said the learning tour was very informative and we are figuring out how we can work together to bring healthy food and grocery stores to these neighborhoods.

Reflect on the results you reported in Exercise 10.3 and think about the costs required to achieve those results and the value they brought to your organization. Capture your thoughts in Exercise 10.4.

EXERCISE 10.4 Create a Cost-Benefit Analysis for Your Organization's Marketing Activities

Activities	Benefits	Costs		Cost of Not Doing the Activity	Value	Notes
		Cost in Money	Cost in Time			
Awareness Activities						
Engagement Activities						

Use this cost-benefit analysis to determine where you want to focus your marketing efforts in the following year. Ideally, the costs spent in time and money on certain activities go down as you build brand equity and get more efficient in your processes. This will free up resources you can spend on new campaigns and efforts to reach more people.

Hopefully this chapter hasn't been too arduous as you've likely evaluated and adjusted your marketing efforts as they were happening, in real time. If people told you that your website's donation page wasn't functioning properly, you likely got it fixed right away. If a campaign garnered a lot of excitement and engagement from your consumers and the press, you likely have made plans to launch it again next year. And if a social media post generated a lot of comments and donations, you likely boosted it or created more like it.

Taking time for evaluation requires discipline. Most creative people love creating and bringing ideas to life. Once a campaign is over, they like to think about the next one. Isn't it more fun to look ahead than to look back? But as discussed above, spending time reflecting and analyzing what elements of your marketing strategy worked the best can help you know what to focus on (or avoid) in the future. Know that many large brands do this review each year to create both annual marketing plans for the following year and longer-term three-year strategies for the near future.

CONNECTING THE DOTS

Review your analysis. Did you see high engagement from a consumer group you hadn't anticipated reaching? Consider adding this group to your 3 C's framework you developed in Chapter 2. Similarly, revisit the frameworks and exercises you completed in each chapter of this book to see if you'd like to make any adjustments given the learnings you uncovered in your evaluation.

Final Thoughts

These 10 chapters have given you a primer on how to approach marketing that drives a social impact. There is so much more to learn on the subjects we covered, but now you know the basics of the frameworks, marketing tactics, and evaluation methods you can employ to start getting your ideas out into the world. While this guidebook has tried to simplify concepts, know that this type of marketing is uniquely challenging. It involves juxtaposition of seemingly opposite ideas:

- ▶ Serious and complex issues (such as climate change and gender equality) must be made engaging and easy to understand

- ▶ A sense of urgency is important, yet long-term, sustained impact takes time

While the work is difficult, you will undoubtedly find it meaningful. And rest assured that there are no right or wrong ways to do marketing, there is just effective and not-so-effective marketing. (Though please take care to be honest and ethical in all the claims, statements, and approaches you take in your marketing efforts. If you aren't honest and ethical in your approach, that's when your marketing would be wrong.)

Finally, thank you. Thank you for thinking up ideas to make a positive impact in the world. And thank you for taking the time to learn how to make these ideas come to life in a way that will be engaging and inspiring. While "Think, Act, Evaluate" is an evergreen process that will serve you well in marketing, cultural norms evolve and therefore marketing tactics will have to change with them. This is what keeps marketing exciting. Enjoy the journey and have fun!

ACKNOWLEDGMENTS

First and foremost, I have to thank my mother for cultivating in me an interest in, and a sense of responsibility around, community service. When I was younger, she took me to beach cleanups, got me to volunteer at the local hospital during my summer vacations, and helped me launch and organize my high school's first Teacher Appreciation Week. When I got my first paycheck from my first real job, she encouraged me to pick a nonprofit to donate a percentage to. Now that I'm a professional, seeing how marketing can be in service of social impact is the result of her upbringing. She proofread every line and every exercise in this book with a critical eye, as only a mother would do.

Next, I have to thank my funny, smart, and socially conscious little sister, Meera, who has self-appointed herself as my "intern for life." As we went through the rounds of editing of this book, she kept me focused on my intention to keep the language simple, approachable, and conversational, which is quite different from the conventional textbooks we learned from. Her smiles, giggles, and questioning when reading this book were my litmus test for if I've presented a concept in a fun, interesting, and honest way. Between her and my mother's constructive feedback, this was definitely a family project.

For her support and encouragement, I'd also like to express my gratitude to my best friend, Lisa Rodriguez. When I told her, "Hey, I think this sounds really nerdy, but I want to write a textbook on social impact marketing. I'll understand if I'm not cool enough to be your bestie anymore," she said, "It's too late for that. We're in this together."

Thank you to my girlfriends and cheerleaders Alisa Baker, Karen Chern, Elina Gorlenkova, Janice Gumera, Mona Jolly, and Sara Verman. Our friendship started when we were learning marketing together at NYU, and I seek their counsel and perspectives when approaching any significant project or campaign.

To John Baird and Noelle Henneman at Kendall Hunt Publishing – thank you for your guidance and hard work in bringing this textbook to life. Thank you to Jyo Pai for offering her wisdom, edits, and love. Thank you to Joe Gray, my brilliant and thoughtful editor, who helped me refine and polish the prose while maintaining my personality and voice.

Writing a textbook on a new subject like social impact marketing means there's a community of professionals who have undertaken this work, so I'd like to acknowledge the changemakers from whom I've taken so much inspiration. We can organize them into three communities:

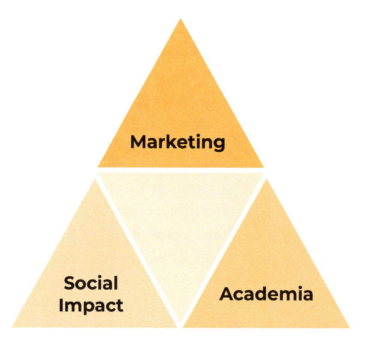

The Marketing Community: Working as a marketer at PepsiCo for over 10 years has shown me what it takes to create billion-dollar global brands. It has also shown me the efforts required to change a system at scale. I joined the company because I admired our then CEO, Indra Nooyi's vision for "Performance with Purpose." Now, CEO Ramon Laguarta is carrying on that legacy with an ambition to develop a more sustainable food system, which I find inspirational. I've also admired the social impact marketing efforts of our peer companies like Unilever, P&G, Nestle, Nike, AB InBev, and others. Big companies are run by individuals, and the individuals who try to leverage the size of a company to make business a force for good, I salute.

The Social Impact Community: I attribute the partners of Social Venture Partners Dallas, and its leader Tony Fleo, with my education in how to organize for impact— through a collaborative effort between nonprofits, business, and government. At the time of this publication, Social Venture Partners has approximately 40 chapters in various cities around the world made up of changemakers who use their professional expertise and personal passion to do good. Please check them out. I'd also like to thank another changemaker, Margery Miller. An author, businesswoman, founder of the Great Girls Network, and my personal oracle, Margery is an example of how to live life vivaciously, on your own terms, and with intention.

The Academic Community: I want to thank Dr. Julie Haworth, the Director of the University of Texas at Dallas Undergraduate Marketing program, for dreaming up this course on social impact marketing and for selecting me to write and launch it. This class has the students apply their marketing skills towards helping local nonprofits over the course of a semester, and it covers their 100 hours of community service pre-requisite for graduation. I admire how our university's business school has thoughtfully designed a way for students to get course credit, get real world experience, and develop a civically engaged mindset right from the beginning of their careers.

And finally, thank you to my students, past, present, and future. I learn so much from you. I look forward to seeing the wonderful social impact you create in this world.

REFERENCES

Introduction

Lifebuoy Arabia. (2013, April 8). *Colour Changing Handwash from Lifebuoy!* [Video]. YouTube. https://www.youtube.com/watch?v=RPslfjjzvJ8

Pallotta, D. (2013, March). *The way we think about charity is dead wrong.* TED Talks. https://www.ted.com/talks/dan_pallotta_the_way_we_think_about_charity_is_dead_wrong

Porter Novelli/Cone. (2019). *Undivided 2019 Gen Z Purpose Study.* https://www.conecomm.com/research-blog/cone-gen-z-purpose-study

Chapter 1

ALS Ice Bucket Challenge Commitments. (n.d.). ALS Association. http://www.alsa.org/fight-als/ice-bucket-challenge-spending.html

Associated Press. (2016, June 16). *Mexican beer brand launches ad campaign against violence* [Press release]. https://www.dailymail.co.uk/wires/ap/article-3643567/Mexican-beer-brand-launches-ad-campaign-against-violence.html

Haircare Unpackaged. (n.d.). Lush. https://www.lushusa.com/stories/article_haircare-unpackaged.html

theHEINEKENcompany. (2017, February 23). *TECATE commercial* [Video]. YouTube. https://www.youtube.com/watch?time_continue=4&v=kCblRaf5dxs

McCarthy, J. (1960). *Basic Marketing: A Managerial Approach.* Irwin.

Naked. (n.d.). Lush. https://www.lushusa.com/stories/article_our-values-naked.html

TECATE, for a Mexico without violence against women. (2017, December 14). Heineken. https://www.theheinekencompany.com/our-sustainability-story/our-progress/case-studies/tecate-mexico-without-violence-against-women

Chapter 2

America's Leading Beverage Companies Unite To Reduce New Plastic Use & Increase Collection Of Their Valuable Bottles Through "Every Bottle Back" Initiative. (2019, October 29). The Recycling Partnership. https://recyclingpartnership.org/everybottleback/

IKEA ISRAEL - 2019) .איקאה ישראל, March 13). *IKEA ThisAbles- The Project* [Video]. YouTube. https://www.youtube.com/watch?v=a0PA_VpLlDw

MCCANN WORLDGROUP. (2020, November 11). *BEHIND THE SCENES: IKEA THISABLES CAMPAIGN* [Video]. YouTube. https://www.youtube.com/watch?v=1eUvSitBo_E

Ohmae, K. (1991). *The Mind Of The Strategist: The Art of Japanese Business*. McGraw-Hill Education.

Chapter 3

May, A. (2019, February 4). *John Legend and Adam Levine change dirty diapers in Super Bowl Pampers ad, singing song by Chrissy Teigen*. USA TODAY. https://www.usatoday.com/story/life/allthemoms/parenting/2019/02/04/adam-levine-john-legend-sing-diaper-song-pampers-super-bowl-ad/2765828002/

Griner, D. (2019, February 4). *John Legend Proudly Tackles a Dad's Duty in Pampers' Musical Celebration of Fatherhood*. Adweek. https://www.adweek.com/creativity/john-legend-proudly-tackles-a-dads-duty-in-pampers-musical-celebration-of-fatherhood/

Starbucks Coffee Company. (2020). *Starbucks 2019 Global Social Impact Report*. https://stories.starbucks.com/uploads/2020/06/2019-Starbucks-Global-Social-Impact-Report.pdf

Starbucks Focuses Hiring Strategy on Veterans and Military Spouses. (2013, June 11). Starbucks. https://stories.starbucks.com/stories/2013/starbucks-focuses-hiring-strategy-on-veterans-and-military-spouses/

Starbucks Military Commitment by the numbers. (2019, August 2). Starbucks. https://stories. starbucks.com/stories/2019/starbucks-military-commitment/

Tomi Jaya. (2019, February 4). *Commercial Ads – Pampers – Stinky Booty Duty feat John Legend, Adam Levine and Chrissy Teigen* [Video]. YouTube. https://www.youtube.com/ watch?v=Z2RLouJOztE

Chapter 4

Lingle, R. (2018, September 18). *Compostable snacks packaging snags bioplastic award for Danimer Scientific, PepsiCo.* Plastics Today. https://www.plasticstoday.com/packaging/ compostable-snacks-packaging-snags-bioplastic-award-danimer-scientific-pepsico

Puntos Limpios. (n.d.). TriCiclos. https://triciclos.net/puntos-limpios/

Russo, K. (2010, October 5). *Frito Lay to Scrap Loud SunChips Bag.* ABC News. https:// abcnews.go.com/Technology/frito-scraps-loud-sunchips-bag/story?id=11806952

The Late Show with Stephen Colbert. (2017, October 14). *Mark Zuckerberg's Cringeworthy "Visit" To Puerto Rico* [Video]. YouTube. https://www.youtube.com/watch?v= ep_xMVlSWoY&sns=em

United Nations. (n.d.). *THE 17 GOALS | Sustainable Development.* SDGS. https://sdgs. un.org/goals

Chapter 5

Cat & Jack Includes Adaptive Apparel to Help Meet the Needs of Even More Kids. (2018, September 5). A Bullseye View. https://corporate.target.com/article/2017/10/cat-and-jack-adaptive-apparel

The Olympic Rings. (n.d.). International Olympic Committee. https://www.olympic.org/ olympic-rings

Stumbo, E. (2018, August 14). *Target's Cat & Jack Line Adds Sensory-Friendly Uniforms.* The Mighty. https://themighty.com/2018/08/target-cat-jack-sensory-friendly-uniforms/

Chapter 6

21/64 & Dorothy A. Johnson Center for Philanthropy. (2013, July). *Next Gen Donors: Respecting Legacy, Revolutionizing Philanthropy*. https://johnsoncenter.org/wp-content/uploads/2020/10/next-gen-donor-report-updated.pdf

Goldseker, S., & Moody, M. (2020). *Generation Impact: How Next Gen Donors Are Revolutionizing Giving* (Updated and Expanded ed.). Wiley.

Chapter 7

Nike stock closes at all-time high in aftermath of Colin Kaepernick ad campaign. (2018, September 13). Yahoo!Sports. https://sports.yahoo.com/nike-stock-closes-time-high-aftermath-colin-kaepernick-ad-campaign-225007582.html

Serena Williams stars in Nike ad celebrating female athletes set to air during Oscars. (2019, February 24). The Washington Post. https://www.washingtonpost.com/sports/2019/02/25/serena-williams-stars-nike-ad-celebrating-female-athletes-set-air-during-oscars/

Chapter 8

Data Report: FIFA World Cup Ad Cost Analysis. (2020, August 11). SQAD Advertising Research Analytics & Planning. https://sqad.com/news-room/sqad_reports/data-report-fifa-world-cup-ad-cost-analysis/

Dua, T. (2020, February 3). *Here are all the Super Bowl commercials that ran in 2020*. Business Insider. https://www.businessinsider.nl/super-bowl-2020-all-the-commercials-that-will-run-in-2020-1?international=true&r=US#amazon-1

GlobalWebIndex. (2020). *Social Flagship Report 2020*. https://globalwebindex.com

Meah, A. (2018, June 3). *35 Inspirational Michelle Obama Quotes On Success*. Awaken The Greatness Within. https://www.awakenthegreatnesswithin.com/35-inspirational-michelle-obama-quotes-on-success/

Schwartz, N. (2020, February 2). *How much does a 2020 Super Bowl commercial cost?* For The Win. https://ftw.usatoday.com/2020/02/how-much-does-a-2020-super-bowl-commercial-cost

Chapter 9

Davis, L. (2013, May 30). *Livestrong Foundation Communications Team Struggles to Overcome Negative Impact of Lance Armstrong.* PRNEWS. https://www.prnewsonline.com/livestrong-foundation-communications-team-struggles-to-overcome-negative-impact-of-lance-armstrong/

Edelman, R. (2020, September 24). *Action Communications: Our New Mission.* Edelman. https://www.edelman.com/insights/action-communications

Praetorius, D. (2011, February 16). *The Red Cross' Rogue Tweet: #gettngslizzerd On Dogfish Head's Midas Touch.* HuffPost. https://www.huffpost.com/entry/red-cross-rogue-tweet_n_824114

Schrotenboer, B. (2016, May 4). *Livestrong adjusts to life without Lance Armstrong.* USA TODAY. https://eu.usatoday.com/story/sports/cycling/2016/05/04/livestrong-cancer-lance-armstrong-donations/83619386/

Solon, O. (2017, October 9). *Mark Zuckerberg "tours" flooded Puerto Rico in bizarre virtual reality promo.* The Guardian. https://www.theguardian.com/technology/2017/oct/09/mark-zuckerberg-facebook-puerto-rico-virtual-reality

Street Grace. (2019, October 21). Porter Novelli. https://www.porternovelli.com/project/street-grace/

Walcher, J. (2013, June 13). *LIVESTRONG's PR Staff Talks Crisis.* J. Walcher Communications. https://jwalcher.com/livestrongpr/

Wasserman, T. (2011, February 16). *Red Cross Does PR Disaster Recovery on Rogue Tweet.* Mashable. https://mashable.com/2011/02/16/red-cross-tweet/?europe=true

Chapter 10

Jaramillo, C. (2017, December 14). *"This is what Dallas needs": Nearly 600 men answer the call to mentor South Dallas students.* Dallas News. https://www.dallasnews.com/news/2017/12/15/this-is-what-dallas-needs-nearly-600-men-answer-the-call-to-mentor-south-dallas-students/

ABOUT THE AUTHOR

MADDY KULKARNI is the Global Marketing Director for Sustainability & Purpose at PepsiCo where she consults marketing leaders on how to connect the organization's sustainability agenda with their consumers through the voice of their brands. Recognized as a 40 Under 40 business leader by Dallas Business Journal, Maddy has served on boards of Social Venture Partners, the Terry Foundation, and the PR Committee of the Dallas Arboretum. She is also the Founder and Executive Director of Dallas Heroes Project, an organization that creates engaging marketing campaigns to drive awareness of the positive impact local heroes and organizations are making in their communities. Maddy earned an M.B.A. from the NYU Stern School of Business, a B.B.A. from the University of Texas at Austin, and now enjoys teaching our next generation of leaders on how marketing can be a force for good through her Social Impact Marketing course at the University of Texas at Dallas.

Printed in the USA
CPSIA information can be obtained
at www.ICGtesting.com
JSHW062334310723
45719JS00001B/1